Exmoor

the making of
an English upland

An England's Past for Everyone paperback

Other titles in this series:

Bristol: Ethnic Minorities and the City 1000-2001

Bolsover: Castle, Town and Colliery

Burford: Buildings and People in a Cotswold town

Codford: Wool and War in Wiltshire

Cornwall and the Cross: Christianity 500-1560

Parham: an Elizabethan House and its Restoration

Sunderland and its Origins: Monks to Mariners

In association with the Exmoor National Park
Authority and Somerset County Council

Exmoor

the making of
an English upland

MARY SIRAUT

with a contribution from
Rob Wilson-North

Phillimore

First published 2009

A Victoria County History publication
Published by Phillimore & Co. Ltd, Madam Green Farm Business Centre,
Oving, Chichester, West Sussex, England in association with the Institute of
Historical Research at the University of London.
www.phillimore.co.uk

© The University of London, 2009

All rights reserved. Except as permitted under current legislation no part of this
work may be photocopied, stored in a retrieval system, published, performed in
public, adapted, broadcast, transmitted, recorded or reproduced in any form or
by any means, without the prior permission of the copyright owner.

ISBN 978-1-86077-597-0

British Library Cataloguing in Publication Data. A cataloguing record for this
book is available from the British Library.

Typeset in Humanist 521 and Minion

We wish particularly to thank the following EPE and VCH staff for their efforts
during the production of this volume:

John Beckett – Director of the Victoria County History
Matthew Bristow – Historic Environment Research Manager
Catherine Cavanagh – Project Manager
Jessica Davies – Production Assistant
Skye Dillon – Education and Skills Manager
Nafisa Gaffar – Finance and Contracts Officer
Mel Hackett – Communications Manager
Dmitri Nemchenko – Web Manager
Neil Penlington – Administrator
Alan Thacker – Executive Editor of the Victoria County History
Kerry Whitston – Publications Manager
Elizabeth Williamson – Architectural Editor of the Victoria County History

Printed and bound in Great Britain

Front cover: *Hill Farming on Exmoor* by Ann Le Bas. The Le Bas family, originally
    Huguenot refugees, have lived on Exmoor for a hundred years. Painting
    reproduced by kind permission of the owners, Mr and Mrs C.J. Phippen.
Back cover: Helicopter rescuing starving sheep on Exmoor. © Corbis.

Contents

Foreword

I am writing this amidst the remains of deep snows which have brought chaos to our region. Drifts in excess of three feet have paralysed Exmoor and are a timely reminder of how harsh this particular English upland can be. In our modern world we are accustomed to our daily life being relatively unchallenging in terms of the environment we face every day. Today we must journey further afield to encounter Nature's savage beauty. This book, however, reminds us all that, in the past, landscapes like Exmoor presented formidable challenges to those who lived and worked in them. Spectacular weather events were undoubtedly a rarity, but Exmoor has thin soils, high rainfall and still suffers from poor communications – all of these factors combine to make farming, or even just living, on Exmoor a harsh and uncomfortable experience.

Ranulph Fiennes
Greenlands
Exford
February 2009

Preface and Acknowledgements

In his novel *Lorna Doone*, subtitled, 'A Romance of Exmoor', R.D. Blackmore uses the thoughts and emotions of the narrator, John Ridd, to give the reader a tangible sense of Exmoor as a place – 'I feel with every blade of grass, as if it had a history'.[1] *Exmoor: The Making of an English Upland* traces that history, from the earliest settlers in prehistory to the present-day communities making a living in a wild and still isolated landscape. But this paperback is only one component of a Heritage Lottery-funded study that explored 11 parishes in southern Exmoor, part of a wider project called 'England's Past for Everyone', which covers 10 English counties. The aim is to enable the Victoria County History to share its knowledge and make its research more widely available through websites, as well as illustrated books, and work with schools and volunteers.

The website accompanying the project, www.ExploreEnglands Past.org.uk/Exmoor, incorporates hundreds of images and short historical articles on a wide range of topics relating to southern Exmoor, past and present.

The southern Exmoor school project was an investigation by Dulverton Middle School into the history and economics of farming and settlement in Exmoor from 1840 to the present day, with an emphasis on the last 60 years. Exmoor is unique in that it has its own school curriculum. As the project incorporates outdoor study, the children were able to practise using maps and surveys and go on a visit to a local farm. They followed this up with discussions, an exhibition and leaflets detailing their findings. Thanks are due to Hilary Binding, the education consultant on the project, former EPE education officer Aretha George, Cloggs Farm, Somerset County Council and Exmoor National Park Authority.

The group of volunteers who worked on the project was led by Anne Todd. They recorded historic farmsteads within the project area, traced abandoned farmsteads using historic maps and census records, and mapped green lanes and old, unmetalled roads that linked the ancient settlements and farms. The data they collected has been entered into a database at the Exmoor National Park Authority and will be invaluable in the future. The project would have been impossible without the dedicated work of Anne Todd and the many volunteers who took part.

Finally, this book could not have been produced without the support of past and present colleagues. Rob Wilson-North, who

wrote chapter 2, Robert Dunning, Spencer Dimmock, Rachel
Thomas and Graham Wills contributed to the research and writing,
while all at the London office provided editorial and production
expertise. The help and support of Somerset County Council's
Heritage Service made the writing of this book possible. Thanks
are also due to Chris Webster of Somerset Historic Environment
for advice on the Dumnonii, Lawrence Bostock for supplying
images from Somerset County Museum collections, the Somerset
Archaeological and Natural History Society for permission to
use their manuscripts and drawings, Peter Collings of Somerset
Record Office for scanning SRO images, and the Somerset Record
Office and depositors for allowing material to be published. Other
photography is by Heather Lowther and Exmoor National Park
Authority staff.

Mary Siraut

*Mary Siraut is a historian and archivist and has worked on the
Victoria County History of Somerset since 1978 as assistant editor and
more recently as county editor. She has also been involved in adult
education and in the cataloguing of many important archives in both
Cambridgeshire and Somerset. The Exmoor project is a partnership
between Somerset County Council, the University of London's Institute
of Historical Research, and the Exmoor National Park.*

[1] R.D. Blackmore, *Lorna Doone: A Romance of Exmoor*
(Wordsworth Classics, 1993), 103.

Chapter 1 | Southern Exmoor

Figure 1 The landscape of southern Exmoor. Photographed from the county boundary at Two Barrows, 1,585 feet above sea level looking into Devon. The early morning mist rising off the lower land in thick layers gives the landscape a mysterious quality.

Exmoor is a name known to many who have never been there. It calls to mind a National Park, deer, ponies, wild moors, and of course *Lorna Doone*. Most people visit by car or coach to gaze upon the moors from the safety of tea rooms or pub gardens, perhaps on their way to or from the coast of Somerset and North Devon. The more adventurous ride, walk or cycle across the moors and stop to watch ponies or deer. Some of the many visitors stay at local hotels, or more commonly in self-catering accommodation and tour the surrounding area. In winter the cold, windswept, frozen, or rain-sodden moors are left largely to the residents.

The study area, for which we have used the term 'southern Exmoor', often seems isolated and insular despite its many summer visitors. Those who live here are often passionate in their love of the area. They define themselves as from Exmoor, rather than Devon or Somerset, even in Brushford, which is outside the National Park. Although Exmoor, defined either as the National Park (265 square miles) or the geographical region, is mainly in Somerset, it has more in common with the counties of Devon and Cornwall.

Figure 2 The study area of Exmoor in the south west of England.

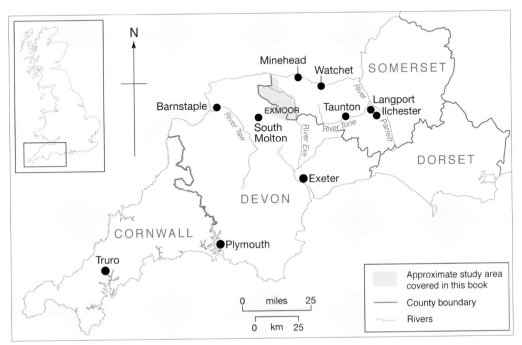

Figure 3 Withypool
post office, shop and
filling station, with
tearooms opposite.

There is a great variety of landscape and settlement on Exmoor and this book focuses on one urban and 10 rural parishes in the southern, inland part of the area including the former Royal Forest. The study area covers the Devon parishes of East and West Anstey, Molland, and Twitchen, and the Somerset parishes of Brushford, Dulverton, Exford, Exmoor, Hawkridge (now joined with Withypool), Winsford, and Withypool. Apart from Brushford, the parishes (in whole or in part) lie within the Exmoor National Park. On occasion, we have also researched beyond these parishes to find comparative material and build a more complete picture for periods where sources are scarce. The book begins with the earliest origins of settlement in prehistory, its agriculture and industries, then focuses on the medieval landscape and its people. The influence of national events such as the Civil War is explored before the evidence for farming, principally from an extensive study of extant buildings, is discussed in detail. Finally, we look at life in Exmoor today and the effect of recent events.

AN UPLAND LANDSCAPE

The Exmoor countryside may give the appearance of being natural, but the landscape we see today is the result of millennia of human intervention, which has left often subtle traces for us to decipher.

Exmoor belongs to the highland zone of Britain and is among the areas regarded as marginal, sharing more of its geography and history with the upland areas of Britain than with the neighbouring lowland. Most of these areas are in the north, including the High Peak and the Lake District, but three lie in the South West, namely Bodmin moor, Dartmoor and Exmoor. They all have similar characteristics such as low temperatures, high rainfall, thin soil, acidity and infertility caused largely by leaching of minerals in heavy rain. The productive season is short and few arable crops can be grown, so livestock rearing is the key to survival and exploitation of wild resources is vital. While transhumance, the use of summer farms on the high ground, was practised in Wales and northern England, it was apparently not in Exmoor, although summer agistment of sheep (grazing on moors, usually for a charge per animal) was common. Rainfall is high and evaporation low, which leads to the formation of bogs and peat and the growth of sedge and cotton grass. Only with enclosure and the development of heavy agricultural machinery did it become possible to cultivate the wetter moors, and then it proved uneconomic except for improved grass.

Many upland areas were rich in game animals, which is why so many were appropriated as Royal Forest, protected from the extension of agricultural land even during periods of population pressure, such as the 13th century. Managed grazing for livestock rearing was the dominant use of the upland and the Royal Forests. From the 17th to the 19th centuries, more profitable cattle and horse breeding partly replaced the great sheep flocks as wool prices fell following enclosure and the separation of herds gradually superseded mixed-stock grazing. Private landownership and controlled breeding produced improved herds and more sophisticated and profitable marketing of animals. Today, sheep still predominate but fewer cattle and horses are kept in the uplands, while Dartmoor and Exmoor retain small pony herds.

From the early Middle Ages a large swathe of the landscape was Royal Forest, the preserve of the privileged hunter and the local poacher. Hunting seemed all the land was fit for in the eyes of outsiders. The Exmoor Forest was an uninhabited expanse of bare moors and bogs with a few tree-lined valleys. In the 1530s John Leland travelled 'From Exford to Simonsbath Bridge four miles, all by forest, barren and moorish ground, where is store and breeding of young cattle but little or no corn or habitation'. He spoke of the Barle which 'when rains come and storms of winter it rages and is deep'. Exmoor was inaccessible for part of the year and even on horseback a man would struggle to reach areas literally off the beaten track. In the 1880s Richard Jefferies described an Exmoor winter as 'eight months with continuous rain and heavy fogs'. For centuries such visitors as were attracted

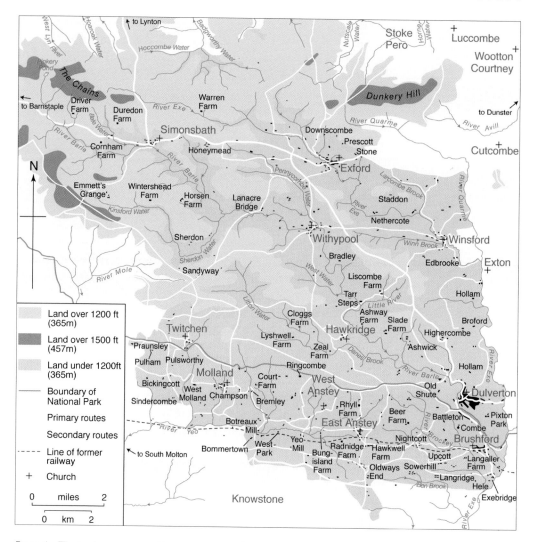

Figure 4 The landscape and settlements of southern Exmoor. The study area includes areas of highland, which were formerly part of Exmoor Forest.

to Exmoor were the privileged classes for whom it was a place to hunt red deer.[1]

People living in upland areas were often regarded either as hardy and self reliant or as wild and uncivilised by lowland dwellers. Extending law enforcement and education was difficult. Monastic communities 'tamed' wild areas in the Middle Ages but unusually Exmoor did not attract orders like the Cistercians. Barlynch and Dunster priories were near Exmoor but were very small communities. After the Reformation the established church often ignored the spiritual needs of upland communities probably because married clergy were reluctant to live in them and found the income inadequate. Upland areas often welcomed Methodists and Bible Christians who used local lay ministers to reach even the smallest communities and were prominent on Exmoor in the late 19th century.

The industrial revolution brought prosperity to some
upland areas, with textile mills taking advantage of the available
waterpower but Exmoor only had a small silk mill; when steam
power replaced water, the area was too remote from a coalfield to
be considered. Transport difficulties also hampered development
as some Exmoor communities had no good roads. However, the
railways liberated many upland areas, including southern Exmoor.
High capital investment and skilled engineering enabled railways to
access remote areas using cuttings, tunnels and viaducts.

Southern Exmoor is bounded on the east by the Quarme and
the Exe and is divided in two by the Barle. The Barle and the Exe
meet just north of Exebridge. The area occupies over 69,000 acres
of which approximately 15,500 acres lie in Devon and 20,344
acres in the former Exmoor Forest. As well as the main rivers,
Litton Water or Dane's Brook divides Devon from Somerset, and
Badgworthy Water drains the northern part of the former forest.
The ancient county and forest boundaries have many markers
across the moors. Leland rode two miles west from Simonsbath
bridge 'up a high moorish hill' and came to the 'span, and the tors;
for there be hillocks of earth cast up of ancient time for marks and
limits betwixt Somersetshire and Devonshire and here about is the
limits and bounds of Exmoor Forest'.[2]

Upland is usually regarded as land over 800 feet and most of
Exmoor lies between 1,000 feet (305 metres) and 1,500 feet (457
metres). The highest point on Exmoor at over 1,700 feet (517
metres) is Dunkery Beacon, to the north-east of the study area. The
moors are divided into ridges running north-west to south-east.
An escarpment, consisting of Anstey, Molland and Withypool
commons, lies between the river Barle, and the Devon Yeo and
straddles the county boundary. It consists largely of Devonian

Figure 5 Exmoor
landscape of heather
moor, improved
grazing and stunted
trees at Nutscale near
Honeycombe Hill. Heath
and moor cover more
than half of
southern Exmoor.

slates, but in the extreme south along the Yeo valley and east as
far as Dulverton are outcrops of limestone, widely quarried. The
main ridge, including the Chains and Winsford Hill, rises to well
over 1,500 feet between the Barle and Quarme valleys, bisected by
the river Exe. The Hangman Grits sandstone here resists erosion
and therefore includes Exmoor's highest points. The high plateau
became the heart of the Royal Forest. The alluvial river valleys cut
across the geology, which is rich in minerals like copper and iron.
On the high ground are large deposits of peat despite extensive
removal over the centuries.

There are few roads in southern Exmoor. The Dunster to Exeter
road follows the eastern boundary and the Taunton to Barnstaple
road skirts the southern boundary. Minor but probably ancient
roads run north from Dulverton over Winsford Hill to Exford
and from Wheddon Cross on the Dunster road through Exford
and Simonsbath to the north Devon coast towns. Exmoor's many
watercourses, often raging torrents in winter, were not navigable and
must have caused problems for earlier inhabitants who relied on
fords. During the Middle Ages most fords were replaced by bridges,
many of which survive although they were largely rebuilt after the
1952 flood. One of the most important river crossings is Dulverton
bridge at the entrance to the only town in southern Exmoor.

Figure 6 Exmoor Land
Rover bus service, 1973.
Attempts have been
made to provide public
transport for local people
and tourists but, apart
from schoolchildren, few
use it.

Figure 7 Exmoor ponies in summer coats. About eight herds are currently managed on Exmoor, two of them by the Park Authority. Southern Exmoor is home to the majority, including the Anchor herd on Winsford hill founded by Sir Thomas Acland in the 18th century.

The railway also played an important part in the development of southern Exmoor for nearly a century but it is motor transport, which has dominated and, many would argue, damaged Exmoor.

Exmoor has a distinctive flora and fauna. Red deer are the largest surviving native animal in England and the Exmoor herd may be the oldest in continuous existence. Although they travel the moors, they tend to keep close to the wooded areas for safety and careful conservation has ensured that there are a couple of thousand animals in the Park. More often seen is the Exmoor pony, one of the oldest wild horses in Europe. Although they have owners, the ponies live wild on the moor all year round and are adapted to their harsh environment, living on gorse when there is no grass. Southern Exmoor is also home to adders, dormice, nightjars, the heath fritillary, wild whitebeam trees and the endangered Ballerina wax-cap toadstool. Its upland habitats include heath and blanket bog as well as unimproved grassland, where the dominant colours are often heather purple and gorse yellow. There are few trees outside the valleys.

Exmoor has traditionally lured the hunter, and its wild beauty must have been admired long before the poets and artists of the Romantic Movement made it fashionable. Others, such as naturalists, miners, farmers and sightseers have also been attracted over the years. But who does Exmoor belong to? Once it was owned by the Crown and now by private landowners, although it is under the management of the National Park. With demands for freedom of access to roam the open countryside, do areas like Exmoor belong to landlords, residents, or the public at large?

WHY SETTLE ON EXMOOR?

The Exmoor upland may seem wild and infertile, but to a farmer it represents valuable grazing, rough or improved. The constant flow of water through the soil down the slopes leaches nutrients, and even the soil itself, to the valley floor. This leads to fertile valley land suitable for arable, hay, and improved grass. Even plants such as bracken and heather were formerly valuable resources, gathered for use round the farm then spread with dung on valley fields. Until the modern period Exmoor supplied stone for building and walling, heather for thatching and bedding, peat, furze and scrub for fuel, game and wild berries and grazing for livestock. The valleys provided shelter, water, fish, timber, meadow and arable.

Why did prehistoric people choose to settle on Exmoor? Was it because the better lands were already occupied or was it safer living on hills, which could be enclosed and defended? Or was it because there were rich mineral resources that could be easily exploited? In historic times population pressure probably drove people deeper into the hills. More recently, a passion for improving on nature, or a romantic love of wild landscapes, has drawn people to Exmoor. For the poor, survival meant mutual co-operation in utilising natural resources. Small hill farmers traditionally relied on supplementary occupations such as quarrying, mining, weaving or estate work. For a large family farming was a part-time occupation and the land could not support them all. The loss of alternative employment at the end of the 19th century meant that many had to leave the land. By the 20th century wealthy businessmen, traditional huntsmen, livestock farmers and poor cottagers had homes on the moor, which they exploited for their own needs.

Were Exmoor people habituated to the moors like the sheep were? Despite the difficulties, most people living on Exmoor, which did at least provide them with almost free food and fuel, wanted to stay. Many could not envisage living away and were unhappy if they had to move. Young people might be forced to leave to look for work, but children often left school as soon as possible to secure

Figure 8 An Exford postman fording the river Exe on his rounds in 1962. Although the area was less isolated than in earlier centuries, getting around Exmoor was still difficult in the mid-20th century.

work locally even though they worked over 12 hours a day for about 10s. a week.

Farmers in particular felt obliged to carry on, whatever their hardships and losses, sometimes putting the farm before family or their own health. 'They belonged to the past; like some old tree they just couldn't survive being uprooted.' They assumed their children would take over the family farm and would marry the children of neighbours. Farm skills were learnt young by helping to feed the stock or milk the cows.[3]

Farmers were not unique; even professional people like teachers would not consider moving far from the moor. In large families, however, work could not be found for all, like the five brothers from Winsford who went to London and joined the police. Oral testimony suggests that many who grew up on the moor regret that their children have had to leave.[4]

Lack of employment and affordable housing has distorted the populations of some Exmoor communities. Ironically people of working age have had to leave and retired people have been able to stay, either because sale of a large property elsewhere has enabled them to buy a village cottage or because they have a house provided by the local authority. The provision of suitable housing and services for the elderly has concentrated the over 65s in Dulverton where they formed 40 per cent of the population recorded in the 2001 census. Just under a third of the populations of Molland, East Anstey and Brushford were over 65, compared with less than 17 per cent in Exmoor parish.

What is the appeal to outsiders? Is Exmoor one of England's last wildernesses? In reality farmers have shaped it in every generation and even wild areas like Winsford hill have been under the plough. Today the deer and ponies are managed. The isolation of the moor is attractive to some although military planes disturb the peace and every village throngs with tourist traffic in the summer. Even with modern conveniences life on the moor is tough in winter when the weather can be ferocious and remote farms can still be cut off from the outside world for periods of time. To Hope Bourne, the writer, such isolation was attractive, but many second home owners would rather winter elsewhere.

Exmoor may often seem like an idea, a dream, an aspiration, a place to enjoy, a national treasure, but it is also a home and a livelihood to a small but significant population. The purpose of this book is to try to discover how the settlement of Exmoor came about and how its farms and villages were developed or abandoned over time and how the people of Exmoor have survived on their often inhospitable upland from prehistory to the 21st century.

Chapter 2

The Earliest Settlement

Figure 9 From within the Bronze-Age hut circle on Honeycombe Hill, the occupants looked out over their fields to the nearby burial mound – the resting place of ancestors.

The remote upland nature of much of Exmoor and its resulting marginality combine to make it one of the richest landscapes, archaeologically, in southern England. These factors ensure the survival of archaeological sites and even quite complex landscapes from the earliest prehistoric periods. Exmoor is one of the few places in England where we can locate our remotest past with some degree of confidence. We can see traces of the periods of prehistory which do not survive well elsewhere; periods that began the process of shaping the English landscape, which we all recognise today.

The span of visible human occupation on Exmoor in prehistory covers the late Mesolithic period (around 6500 BC) to the time of the Roman occupation of Britain (AD 43) and beyond. In social terms, it ranges from late-Mesolithic groups of hunter gatherers to a completely settled, organised and formally stratified society at the end of the Roman period. The archaeological evidence does not, however, provide a seamless story of Exmoor's prehistoric communities. Rather it leads us to a sequence of pictures – some very detailed indeed – which move us forward through the millennia; the episodic richness of the evidence is equalled by the challenge of the gaps in the record.

HUNTER GATHERERS

To understand the origins of human settlement we must look back before the arrival of the first people. The landscape had been marked by the last Ice Age, which finally relinquished its grip on the South-West around 10,000-9000 BC. That is not to say that ice sheets ever covered Exmoor. Rather this landscape lay at the frontier of the ice: a place of periglacial trauma characterised by bouts of freezing and thawing and mud slides creating a shattered, inhospitable landscape. As the climate warmed, people returned, but apparently not to Exmoor until after 8000 BC. The archaeological record is silent for the early Mesolithic period on Exmoor, but there is good evidence of human activity at Westward Ho! (North Devon) and on Mendip (Somerset). By 7000 BC, during the late Mesolithic period, the landscape had recovered from barren, semi-frozen tundra to mixed deciduous woodland with some pine forest on the higher ground. Only the very highest parts of Exmoor were not

This chapter is by Rob Wilson-North, archaeologist for the Exmoor National Park Authority.

11

forested. Groups of hunter gatherers moved across this wooded landscape and provide the first evidence of people on Exmoor in the shape of occasional flint finds and, at Hawkcombe Head near Porlock, the remains of occupation.

Hawkcombe Head

Hawkcombe Head lies close to the Exmoor coast at 1,355 feet (413 metres) above sea level. Late Mesolithic flints have been found here since the 1940s and comprise small microliths, which were used to tip arrow hafts, blades and other tools. In 2001 a field survey, fieldwalking, geophysical survey and excavation were carried out

Figure 10 A Timeline detailing the phases of visible occupation on Exmoor in prehistory.

DATE	PERIOD	SOCIAL	EVIDENCE	EXAMPLE SITES ON EXMOOR
10,000 BC – 8000 BC	Early Mesolithic	Small hunter gatherer groups	Flint tools, maceheads	-
8000 BC – 4000 BC	Late Mesolithic	Small hunter gatherer groups	Flint tools; woodland clearance	Hawkcombe Head; Porlock Beach
4000 BC – 3000 BC	Early Neolithic	Origins of farming; semi settled communities	Causewayed enclosures; long barrows; henge monuments	-
3000 BC – 2000 BC	Late Neolithic	Origins of farming; semi settled communities	Stone monuments	East Pinford stone setting;
2000 BC – 700 BC	Bronze Age	Mainly/entirely settled communities	Stone monuments; barrows; hut circles and field systems	Standing stones, stone settings and stone circles; Wambarrows; East Anstey Barrows
700 BC – AD 43	Iron Age	Highly stratified, tribal society	Enclosures; hillforts;	Cow Castle; Mounsey Castle; Oldberry Castle; Bat's Castle; Timberscombe hillfort
AD 43 – AD 410	Roman	Increasingly productive, organised and urban society	Roman military sites; iron working sites	Old Burrow and Martinhoe fortlets; Roman Lode; Sherracombe Ford iron smelting site
AD 410 – AD 1066	Early Medieval	Upheaval; population movements; instability	-	-

Figure 11 Map showing selected prehistoric and Roman sites located within Exmoor National Park in relation to modern settlements.

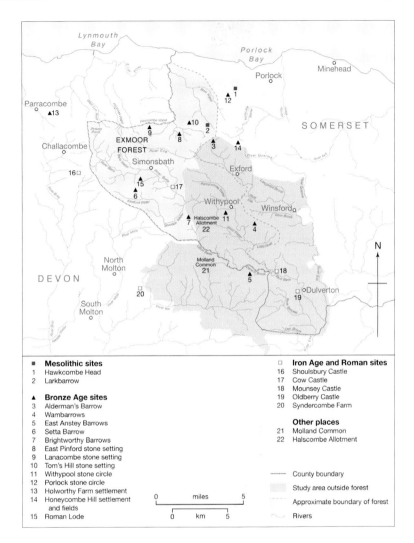

	Mesolithic sites			Iron Age and Roman sites
1	Hawkcombe Head	16	Shoulsbury Castle
2	Larkbarrow	17	Cow Castle
		18	Mounsey Castle
▲	**Bronze Age sites**	19	Oldberry Castle
3	Alderman's Barrow	20	Syndercombe Farm
4	Wambarrows		
5	East Anstey Barrows		**Other places**
6	Setta Barrow	21	Molland Common
7	Brightworthy Barrows	22	Halscombe Allotment
8	East Pinford stone setting		
9	Lanacombe stone setting		
10	Tom's Hill stone setting		County boundary
11	Withypool stone circle		
12	Porlock stone circle		Study area outside forest
13	Holworthy Farm settlement		
14	Honeycombe Hill settlement		Approximate boundary of forest
	and fields		
15	Roman Lode		Rivers

by the University of Bristol and Exmoor National Park Authority. This work revealed traces of temporary, short-lived occupation. Scatters of worked flints, two hearths and a probable structure have been found close to the springheads at Hawkcombe Head itself and at Ven Combe to the west. This suggests that people came here as part of their exploitation of the high forested hills, and in particular of the red deer that would have lived there. Radiocarbon dates obtained from charcoal fragments within a hearth and from a posthole suggest that occupation was in the period 6500-6000 BC: the late Mesolithic period.

Sea levels were never constant and fluctuated throughout the Mesolithic period. By 5000 BC they were within six-and-a-half feet (two metres) below their present level. It seems likely that these hunter gatherers would have spent most of their time on this

Figure 12 Looking from Exmoor to the Severn Plain in the Mesolithic period, when sea levels were 98-131 feet (30-40 metres) lower than today. From Hawkcombe Head people would have looked out over a gentler coastline with extensive grassland and a wooded plain stretching away to the River Severn in the far distance.

abundant yet evolving coastal plain, with less frequent visits to the higher ground. While there is no direct evidence for woodland management on Exmoor during the Mesolithic period, it seems highly likely that from time to time the woods were deliberately burned or that natural openings in the canopy were exploited. This would have encouraged grazing by wild animals and, as a consequence, these places would have become hunting glades for groups of hunter gatherers. No doubt these activities combined with a cooling of the climate to cause a decline in woodland cover and the emergence of blanket bog on the very high ground around 4500-4000 BC. Managing the woodlands represented an investment of time and effort in particular locations, and it is partly through such activities that the concept of ownership evolves. It is impossible to say whether anything as formal as territories existed at this time, but it is likely that several groups would have had a vested interest in the high ground of Exmoor. These groups may have been drawn from the 'Severn Plain' and from the Exe valley and the tributary valleys of the River Taw. The upland of Exmoor was perhaps an important but infrequently exploited resource, and hunting there brought particular rewards. Locations like Hawkcombe Head were significant for hunting and other activities, which occurred on Exmoor.

Hunter gatherers on Exmoor in the late Mesolithic period probably lived in groups of between 10 and 30 individuals. Their nomadic lifestyles and the difficulties faced by pregnant and lactating women as the family hunted over a wide area hindered reproduction and hence limited population. Britain as a whole had perhaps only some 24,400 inhabitants during this period. This figure, which equates to one person per six to twelve miles, would mean that Exmoor's population would have been around fifty people (in 2001 it was 10,873). While such estimates are inevitably speculative and fail to take into account local circumstances, they give us some insight into the predominantly uninhabited landscape of the time.[5]

Evidence of Mesolithic activity on Exmoor is scarce, but it represents the momentous, gradual and poorly understood first steps towards human management and eventual manipulation of the entire landscape. Mesolithic traditions from elsewhere reveal relationships between people, with the world around them and with the animals that inhabited it. We have a handful of intimate pictures of these relationships, including the survival of skeletal material from the Mendips, or further afield, from the burial of a woman with a newborn child laid on a swan's wing from Vedbæk in Denmark or the find of human hand bones upon a seal's flipper bones from Oronsay off the west coast of Scotland. All of which suggests a particular relationship with the animal kingdom and its water-loving species.[6]

Another insight into Exmoor's Mesolithic world may perhaps be gained through consideration of the impact of rising sea levels. It may well be that the area was exploited in the late Mesolithic period, and not before, because of the changing pressures on coastal communities with the inundation of the extensive 'Severn Plain' to form the present Severn Estuary. For such communities rising sea levels made a closer relationship with Exmoor inevitable. Their response to these pressures perhaps looks forward to the Neolithic period – the New Stone Age – when the

Uncovering Exmoor's Prehistoric Past

Figure A   Withypool stone circle (right of centre) in an island of survival amongst areas of medieval ridge and furrow cultivation on Withypool Hill. The circle was discovered in 1898 and is approximately 118 feet in diameter. Originally consisting of around 100 stones, the 37 that survive are most clearly visible against the blackened earth following 'swaling' or burning of the moorland heather.

The landscape of southern Exmoor contains a wealth of prehistoric remains, surviving best within the former Royal Forest and around its margins. Here, the land has hardly been cultivated since the Bronze Age – except where 19th-century reclamation and improvement have taken place – and we are able to discern the complex remains of early prehistoric communities. South of the Royal Forest, the commons were ploughed in the medieval period and still contain vast tracts of ridge and furrow, which has obliterated all but the most enduring prehistoric features or chance survivals between these later areas of cultivation. Further away still the network of farms and fields, which has its origins in the early medieval period, has almost entirely effaced the prehistoric pattern. Only the most obdurate burial mounds have not been levelled. However, traces of the earlier landscapes from time to time do emerge, and will continue to do so as archaeological techniques improve. Taken together the landscape of southern Exmoor conveys a story of continual settlement

Figure B   Collecting peat cores from a valley mire system on Molland Common.

expansion and contraction around the moors as climatic, economic and social circumstances permitted.

Evidence for past environments is contained within many buried archaeological deposits, but upland peat bogs and valley mires are especially rich locations. They contain a stratified record of flora and fauna which is highly detailed and crucially, datable, through Carbon 14 dating methods. In a sense they are a chronological document, or archive, of environmental change. The ratio of Carbon 14, a radioactive isotope, to carbon in living organisms diminishes after death at a measurable rate providing a guide to the date of death. Researching this archive requires a particular combination of fieldwork and laboratory skills. On Halscombe Allotment the remains of an ancient oak tree were discovered during archaeological fieldwork and were subsequently dated to c.5400 BC by Carbon 14 dating. The oak tree came from a valley mire and was found at the foot of a face of peat five feet three inches deep. Subsequent sampling and analysis of this peat deposit revealed a build up of peat from the late Mesolithic period onwards. At that time the area was densely wooded, but subsequently the tree cover gradually declined until, around 2000 BC, there was a rapid removal of woodland and the establishment of grassland management systems for livestock. The peat at Halscombe Allotment eloquently tells the story of a changing environment and human endeavour.

Figure C   *A typical Exmoor valley mire at Colley Water. These areas of waterlogged deep peat preserve a wealth of archaeological deposits crucial for understanding prehistoric life on Exmoor.*

construction of monuments and mankind's formal appropriation
of the landscape began.

The transition from a hunter gatherer lifestyle to one that
is centred on agricultural production is poorly understood.
It is likely that Mesolithic communities in Britain acquired
domesticated animals and plants and the means to cultivate
them from Europe, where agriculture had been developed, but
the date and method of change are still unclear. The speed at
which farming was adopted is uncertain, but where there were
no pressures on space it seems most likely that the transition was
gradual. On Exmoor, chance flint finds in the form of leaf-shaped
and transverse arrowheads indicate that people still used Exmoor
as a hunting ground in the Neolithic period. The region is notable
for the absence of the characteristic communal monuments of
the early Neolithic period such as causewayed enclosures and,
their south-western moors equivalents, the tor enclosures. Absent,
too, are the burial monuments of the period: the long barrows,
long cairns and chambered tombs. All this perhaps suggests
that Exmoor was not occupied intensively in the early Neolithic
period, but continued as a wooded upland, valuable from time
to time as a hunting area. Certainly around Exmoor, woodland
passed through a period of, perhaps natural, decline during the
fourth millennium BC, but subsequently recovered. There is little
evidence for human activity at this time. On the northern edge of
Molland Common there seems to have been a phase of woodland
decline during the Mesolithic/Neolithic transition, and it has been
suggested that this represents the sporadic activities of hunter
gatherers, although much more work needs to be done before this
can be asserted with confidence.[7]

Figure 13   Hunting tools
from the late Mesolithic
and Neolithic periods
show typological and
technological advances,
but perhaps they also
reflect the continuing use
of Exmoor as an upland
hunting ground.

0   20mm

APPROPRIATION: MONUMENTS AND FARMING

As the Neolithic Age progressed changes to the climate, and, possibly to social organisation as well, meant that elsewhere in southern England causewayed enclosures and long barrows were abandoned in favour of henges, circles of stones and rows of stones (sometimes called 'avenues'). Stone circles can be seen as 'part of the increasingly elaborate landscapes of the later Neolithic'. Many, including Stonehenge, are the culmination of several phases of building. On Exmoor, for the first time, monuments were built which corresponded with examples from elsewhere, allowing comparison with other places. They are the first built structures that still survive. Of the 13 stone circles in Somerset, two are on Exmoor; at Porlock Allotment and on Withypool Hill. Neither, in common with most of Exmoor's standing stone monuments, are impressive structures. In fact, the circle on Withypool Hill was only found when, in 1898, Mr Archibald Hamilton's horse tripped on one of the stones lurking in the heather. The circles may well have been associated with observances and rituals relating to solar events, although, in the case of the Withypool circle, the tiny size of the stones can have been of little practical value. As such, stone circles may be seen as being of key relevance to a local community and would have lain at the metaphorical, if not the physical heart of it.[8]

Thought to be of similar date are the stone rows or avenues, of which there are eight on Exmoor. But Exmoor's 'avenues' hardly 'link specific monuments … or provide a grand ceremonial entrance to them', which is the usual view of such structures. While the Porlock stone circle is associated with a double row, the stones are no more than eight inches in height, and so not exactly 'a grand ceremonial entrance'. The White Ladder, discovered in 1975, has only recently re-emerged from the peat, because of the dry summers in 2005 and 2006, to reveal the insubstantial double thread of white quartz and sandstone lumps, which give the site its name. More abundant are Exmoor's stone settings, which have been described by Aubrey Burl as 'delicate stones arranged in geometrical patterns, almost without parallel in Britain and Ireland'. Around sixty complete examples survive, and many more are fragmentary or have been lost completely. The function of Exmoor's stone settings still remains a mystery, but they can at least be said to be part of the tradition of monument building that included the circles and rows.[9]

All of this evidence points towards the formal appropriation by local communities of Exmoor's landscape through the construction of monuments, perhaps beginning during the third

millennium BC. Their diminutive scale may, at first sight, seem
to contradict the notion of appropriation and has often been
explained in terms of the available local stone. But there are also
truly megalithic structures on Exmoor, such as the impressive Long
Stone near Challacombe (nearly 13 feet high) and the great slabs
of the Whit Stones near Porlock. The construction of insubstantial
monuments of standing stones may be explained by their situation.
Although now found on open moorland, which emphasises their
tiny scale, they may have been built in a still-wooded landscape,

Figure 14 The East
Pinford stone setting as it
may have looked whilst
being built. It is one of 60
stone settings on Exmoor,
which form a remarkable
survival beyond the limits
of later cultivation.

perhaps in glades among the trees. Recent work by Mark Gillings and Josh Pollard has shown that stone settings at East Pinford, Tom's Hill and on Lanacombe lie in areas where bedrock is close to the surface. This may have caused limited tree growth and a resultant natural glade in the woodland and maybe even a spring. Today at East Pinford and on Lanacombe the stone settings stand amidst an area of natural surface stone, much of it poking an edge through the turf. Perhaps these stone settings at least were erected to mimic emergent natural features.[10]

Farmsteads and Barrows

The abundance of these stone monuments indicates a very active population, and it is not surprising to find that by the beginning of the second millennium BC (around and after 2000 BC), the woodland cover declined sharply and local people focused increasingly on grassland management. The landscape of Exmoor was becoming a network of farmsteads in which cleared areas were grazed, and sometimes cultivated, while beyond were areas of uncleared or semi-cleared woodland and heath. Settlements comprised small groups of one, two or three round buildings, often within enclosed yards but, equally often, on the open hillsides. Such 'hamlets' would have extended across the whole of Exmoor, and are even found sporadically within the very high ground of what, in medieval times, would become the Royal Forest. The small scale of these settlements is in contrast to Dartmoor and Bodmin and may indicate a different social organisation and local autonomy. Only one settlement site has been excavated on Exmoor, at Holworthy near Parracombe. Work here has revealed middle Bronze-Age activity: charred grain, flints, a loom weight, a charred wooden bowl, Bronze-Age pottery and a quern stone for grinding corn. This all points towards a settled, domesticated lifestyle.[11]

The settlements are often accompanied by traces of fields, and these seem to represent sometimes well planned and sometimes less well structured pieces of land in which crops could be grown and livestock managed. The low stony banks, which separate these fields, must have been topped with long-since decayed hedges in order to make them stock-proof.

Never far away from these Bronze-Age settlements are the still obvious round barrows. Exmoor has over 400 of these monuments, most of which are presumed to date from the early Bronze Age; some may be earlier, while some were built in the middle Bronze Age and even later. Round barrows were burial mounds, often for several individuals and sometimes used over long periods of time. But they were also much more than cemeteries for Bronze-Age people. In southern Exmoor, Brightworthy Barrows, Alderman's Barrow, Wambarrows, Anstey Barrows and Setta Barrow are just a few examples of those that form landmarks and boundaries in the modern landscape, as they have since they were first built. Many lie along Exmoor's long ridges, whilst others lie on the slopes and are found nearer to the settlements and to other monuments. Elsewhere, burial mounds are sometimes only the final and visible culmination of previous rituals and events, and have even been interpreted as part of an event marking the end of the use of that place for such purposes.[12]

Exmoor's barrows are built of available local materials: turf, earth and stone. Some are small and would have been simple to build, but the construction of the larger ones would have

Figure 15 In 1889 a low barrow mound at North Molton was being ploughed when the plough horse, Darling, dropped its hoof into a probable cist or grave within the barrow. A rich necklace of faience beads, lignite, shale and amber was revealed, a selection of which are displayed here.

required considerable effort from the local population. Several Exmoor barrows contain white quartz blocks, which were intended to be highly visible in the completed monument. The use of quartz and other unusual materials in barrow building is a phenomenon observed beyond Exmoor. Quartz is widely available on Exmoor, where it tends to occur locally in the country rock. But it may be that its use was more than for its gleaming whiteness, as it usually occurs with copper in the mineral-bearing lodes that cross the region. At nearby Roman Lode, the presence of deliberately crushed quartz in deposits dating to about 1800 BC shows that the local Bronze-Age people were aware of the potential and value of quartz for the minerals it contained. Perhaps quartz was used in barrows not just for its whiteness but also for what it represented, the technological innovations made possible through the discovery of copper and, subsequently, bronze.[13]

Few Exmoor barrows have been excavated, but a small mound at Bratton Down contained the vestiges of a wooden coffin placed over the burial. Barrows not only contained the dead, but they also defined ownership of the landscape. On ridges they emphasised watersheds, and as such relate to the natural topography and its resources. In settlements they were visible reminders of ancestors or, maybe specifically, individuals who had significance for that community. On Honeycombe Hill, the site of the doorway of a solitary roundhouse faces uphill towards a nearby barrow lying just outside the settlement and its fields. The mound is revealed from the house through a deliberate gap in the nearby contemporary fieldbank; and elsewhere a fieldbank is aligned on the barrow itself. This contrived arrangement ensured that from within the roundhouse the doorway framed the view to the barrow, and this provided a constant link between the world of the living and that of the dead.[14]

THE DUMNONII: ELITES, TERRITORY AND INDUSTRY

At Holworthy, near Parracombe, excavated over three seasons from 2003 to 2005, the archaeology reveals a complicated chronological sequence. It begins with middle Bronze-Age occupation, which left ephemeral traces but was probably predominantly domestic in character, and culminated in Iron-Age re-occupation. Elsewhere there is a wider regional pattern of open settlements in the Bronze Age, giving way to more substantially defined settlement sites during the Iron Age, known to archaeologists as hill-slope enclosures or rounds, depending on whether one is in

Somerset/Devon or Cornwall. On and around Exmoor these small enclosures, although largely unexcavated, are generally thought to be of Iron-Age date and some may continue into and beyond the Roman period. The function of hill-slope enclosures undoubtedly varied, but they are thought to relate to farming or possibly industry. Also from that period are larger enclosures or hillforts, of which there are seven on Exmoor.[15]

What does all this enigmatic and incomplete local archaeological evidence say about the societies and tribal groupings, which it represents? It hampers a fuller understanding of Iron-Age settlement and society but suggests a highly-structured society in which settlements were strongly constructed to express an emphatic presence in the landscape. The pairing of some enclosures, which occurs a number of times on Exmoor, such as the groups at Sweetworthy and at Rodhuish Common, has been taken as evidence of partible inheritance (a system under which property can be shared between heirs). This demonstrates a close connection, perhaps familial, with well defined parcels of land or sub-territories.[16]

The great variety in the size, location and form of the enclosures perhaps arises from their differing dates, social status and function. Their complexity makes it very difficult to reconstruct the pattern of land ownership, but we can perhaps say a little more about what these enclosures were for. Hillforts seem to have had a different function to hill-slope enclosures. Some hillforts, like Cow Castle, may have operated as central places, markets or the focus of socio-political activity between groups. Others, like Mounsey Castle or Oldberry Castle overlooking Dulverton may have contained some settlement and may also have been sited in relation to river crossings or to the availability of raw materials, such as iron ore. A further group, including Wind Hill at Countisbury or Bat's Castle near Dunster, may have had wider strategic functions, dominating coastal resources or providing a visible presence on tribal frontiers (in the case of Bat's Castle, between the Dumnonii to the west and the Durotriges to the east). As the climate deteriorated, becoming wetter and cooler, a stronger grip on resources and land may have been an economic necessity.

Who were the people who created the early settlements on Exmoor? For most of prehistory we know little about them, but by the Iron Age, Exmoor, along with most of south-west England, was inhabited by people who formed part of an identifiable tribal group, the Dumnonii. Their name is Celtic, possibly meaning 'we of this land' and hence being the way they referred to themselves. They were recorded by the Roman geographer, Ptolemy, writing in the early second century when they had several settlements, including Exeter. Regarded as culturally impoverished, the Dumnonii were distinctive in their use of hill slopes and spurs for the construction of simple enclosures, which contrast with the elaborate hill forts found further east. These upland enclosures may relate to a livestock-based economy in which animals were used as currency. That would have suited Exmoor, which was by this date good grazing land.[17]

As part of the conquest of Britain, in the middle of the first century, the Romans established a legionary fortress at Exeter, named by them, *Isca.* The Dumnonii probably resisted the invasion. Small Roman fortlets established around the fringe of Exmoor may be linked to the suppression of pockets of resistance, the subjugation of the tribal aristocracy or the protection of trade, especially in iron ore. From the late first century it would seem that the Dumnonii were incorporated into the Roman province of Britannia, as the *Civitas Dumnoniorum.* Many, at least among the aristocracy and in the principal settlements, adopted Roman ways. The mass of the people, however, probably remained unaffected by the political changes and perhaps continued to identify with a local ruling clan.

In general the Romans left little impression on Exmoor. Pollen analysis shows a continuity of pastoral farming in the uplands since the Iron Age and no evidence of abandonment of land. The Dumnonii, who perhaps administered the area for them re-emerged as a political power after the Romans withdrew from Britannia in the early fifth century. They appear to have formed a cohesive entity under a chief or king and a landowning aristocracy, controlling the area between Land's End and the Quantocks and

Figure 16 This Iron-Age bronze bowl, discovered at a farm in Rose Ash, Devon, on the edge of Exmoor, may have been a religious offering placed in what was then a small spring or marsh some time between 100 BC and AD 100. A detail of the bowl's single handle shows that it was made in the shape of an animal's head, possibly a cow or an ox.

Blackdown Hills. Later kings of Dumnonia, with names such as Constantine (early sixth century) and Gerontius (Geraint, c.700), may have been members of an established and Romanised dynasty of tribal leaders.[18]

While the development of settlement on Exmoor during the Iron Age is still largely unknown, the exploitation of iron has been extensively studied. It is clear that the mining and processing of iron on and around Exmoor was a significant influence in the development of the landscape from the very beginning of the Roman period, although evidence for iron smelting in the pre-Roman Iron Age remains elusive. By the Roman period, trading networks were bringing pottery to Exmoor from other parts of the South West and beyond. Iron smelting enterprises seem to have differed in scale and efficiency, perhaps reflecting different motivations for production. The close spatial relationship between hill forts and iron ore deposits can be demonstrated at Oldberry Castle, with Blacklake Wood iron smelting site; at Mounsey Castle, with later iron mining and smelting near Hinam and at Shircombe Slade respectively; at Cow Castle, with later iron mining at and around Pickedstones; Wind Hill, where later iron mining is visible within the hillfort ramparts, and, to a lesser extent, at Shoulsbury Castle, with mining and smelting at Roman Lode, Hangley Cleave and Sherracombe Ford respectively.[19]

To what extent did the hillforts and enclosures of the Iron Age and Roman periods influence early medieval settlement on Exmoor? And are these places the key to understanding later settlement development? The answer to these questions is by no means clear and the evidence presents a tantalisingly incomplete and at times contradictory picture. Oldberry Castle, near Dulverton, perhaps influenced the development of the medieval town of Dulverton itself; after all it overlooks the town and its river crossing. Elsewhere, iron ore and a hillfort do not seem to have fostered the development of later settlement. Many hill slope enclosures seem to lie away from later farmsteads and roads. Rather than being seen as integral to settlement development are they, rather, cul-de-sacs in the story, dead ends or failed sites? Or should we instead see beneath the superficiality of where a settlement actually is, and focus on what it is there for? Were these enclosures along with many of the lobe shaped enclosures of land (some of which still carry the *worthy* place-name element) viable land units with farmable land, water and other key resources? Have the farmers simply relocated their farmsteads within their holdings? Was the Iron Age and Roman period the beginning of a tenacious bond between local people and the land of Exmoor – Exmoor beneath our feet – and as such the beginning of the settlement pattern we see today?

Figure 17 A
reconstruction showing
Roman iron smelting
at Black Lake Wood
near Dulverton.

It may be that an early medieval farmstead, an Iron-Age
enclosure, and a hillfort lie within a single aristocratic estate.
Changing climate, methods of agriculture, social and trading
patterns and systems of administration may have caused the
chief settlement of an estate to move, but within an ancient estate
boundary. The provision for Britons in the later laws of the Anglo-
Saxon King Ine (688-726) indicates that many were substantial
landowners. It is at least possible that there was continuity in the
estate pattern on Exmoor from Iron Age to Norman Conquest.

Chapter 3

The Anglo-Saxon Centuries

Figure 18 The fine Romanesque south doorway of Hawkridge church. The zig-zag hood moulding suggests that this doorway dates from the early 12th century, one of a small number of surviving Norman architectural features in southern Exmoor.

How did southern Exmoor make the transition from the Iron-Age British landscape with its hillforts and hill-slope enclosures to become part of the medieval counties of Devon and Somerset with their manors, parish churches and small villages? There are very few places where continuity of settlement can be shown from the Iron Age and we know little about British farmsteads. Exmoor is a marginal area, yet also the meeting place of different systems of land use.

By the 11th century, Exmoor's estates were held by kings and their relatives and officials. Domesday Book, a comprehensive survey of manorial assets in England for the purposes of taxation, reveals that by 1086 about two thirds of southern Exmoor belonged to the king, including the forest, Dulverton, Winsford, Molland and North Molton. Was this the result of the Anglo-Saxon and Norman conquests or was there an older connection between Exmoor and kingship, perhaps stretching back to the Bronze Age and late Neolithic period? Did the necklace found at North Molton, an Anglo-Saxon royal manor, belong to Bronze-Age royalty?[20]

THE COMING OF THE WEST SAXONS

In the early 7th century the West Saxons attacked the British kingdom of Dumnonia, which had emerged in the fifth and sixth centuries. Its territory spanned all of Cornwall, Devon and west Somerset as far east as the Quantock and Blackdown Hills, including Exmoor. The West Saxons appear to have met a lot of British resistance before taking control of Exeter, probably in the 670s, but they may have taken Exmoor earlier than this to protect their approach from the north. By the early eighth century the kingdom of Dumnonia, then ruled by Geraint, was contracting and may well have been reduced to Cornwall. The rest of the South-West, including southern Exmoor, became part of the Anglo-Saxon kingdom of Wessex. During the next 350 years the foundations of the modern English state were laid.

British Survival

How far the British population of Exmoor, its settlements and estate patterns, survived the West Saxon conquest remains uncertain.

Place Names of Exmoor

Most Exmoor place names are of Old English origin and represent features of the landscape, such as Hawk*ridge* and Withy*pool*, or means of communication like Brushford (causeway ford), Exford, Dulverton (the settlement by the hidden ford), and Twitchen (the cross road). The Ansteys were named for a strategic trackway, possibly that from Oldway on the county boundary to Molland and North Molton.

Farmsteads might be named after a valley, hill, hollow, tree, or hanger (a wooded slope). Valleys derive their names from their nature or from the animals there. Smallacombe in Molland was narrow and Liscombe in Dulverton had a 'loose' (pigsty). Such

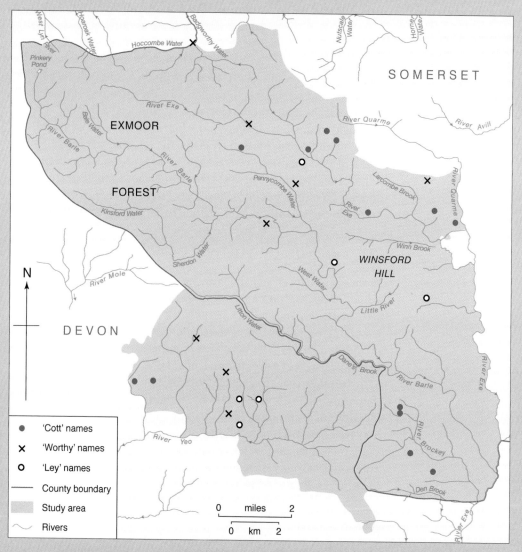

Figure A *Showing distribution of 'cott', 'ley' and 'worthy' names in southern Exmoor. In southern Exmoor 'cotts' and 'worthys' are clustered in the far south and north-east, perhaps indicating that the British had long farmed the central valleys.*

Figure B   *Sindercombe Farm, Twitchen, built on an Iron-Age slag heap. Iron workers were recorded at North Molton in 1086, and there were later iron mines in Molland.*

Figure C   *The ford through the Winn at Winsford on the road out of the village to Withypool, still in daily use, with a footbridge for pedestrians. Most 'ford' names are associated with larger settlements and the emphasis remains on the 'ford' element of names.*

names may be English translations of the older British. The suffix 'combe', a short, steep valley, is used in English and in Welsh as cwm. Many names refer to water, revered by Celtic peoples, such as Hawkwell (crooked stream), Dulverton, Wellshead, or Ludslade (valley of the torrent), Exford. The rivers Exe and Barle have British names meaning 'water' and 'hill stream' respectively. Woodland is recorded in Allshire, Brushford and Ashott, Exford, both derived from shaw (coppice), and Halsgrove, Withypool. Other farm names include acre, ham, hay (enclosed land), hill, land, moor, and marsh.

Names ending in 'cott', 'ley' (leah, a glade) or 'worthy' indicate Anglo-Saxon settlement or places taken over by them. They are common in north Devon and west Somerset but rare in south Devon. That may be due to different phases in the expansion of Wessex, possibly involving settlers with different language or dialects. 'Worthy' names are often attached to large farms, believed to be early Anglo-Saxon, which may have utilised late prehistoric intakes from moorland. Their prefixes are often personal names such as Almsworthy and Buckworthy named after Ealhmund and Bucca. Personal names are otherwise rare on Exmoor except in the Ansteys. Wine gave his name to Winsford, Hroda to Radnidge (Hroda's ash) in East Anstey, and Badda and Hringa to Badlake and Ringcombe in West Anstey. 'Cotts', smaller and later than 'worthys', possibly mark a period of expansion. The 'ley' names are mainly in Molland, a well-wooded parish, including Bremley (bramble glade), and around Winsford Hill. 'Wick' (wic farm or dairy) may indicate a Romano-British farm. Ashwick in Dulverton lies above the bend in the river Barle defended by the twin hillforts of Brewers and Mounsey castles.

The name Molland is unusual and appears to be of Irish origin, meaning 'heap land'. The same word, 'moll', occurs in North and South Molton. It may refer to slag heaps from early iron workings. A large Iron-Age smelting site has been studied at Sherracombe Ford on the northern boundary of North Molton parish near Exmoor Forest and there is Iron-Age slag south of Twitchen.

Figure 19 Penny of King Cnut 1030-5, struck by Godchild the moneyer of Watchet. The mint, close to Exmoor, struck coins for Anglo-Saxon and Norman kings.

While the language change from British to English is clear evidence of the conquerors' cultural dominance, it is nevertheless very likely that a British population survived. The area's place names are no longer thought to be of purely Anglo-Saxon (English) origin. The new landlords and their people probably farmed alongside enclaves of Brittonic speakers, who survived well after the West Saxon takeover, either as tenants or slaves. The laws of the West Saxon king, Ine, drawn up in the early eighth century, distinguish between Anglo-Saxon and British subjects at every social level, from noble to slave, discriminating against the conquered British. Many Anglo-Saxon slaves were probably Britons taken captive during periods of invasion and expansion. The word *walh* (Briton) was sometimes used as a synonym for slave. Although these ethnic distinctions had disappeared by the later ninth century, the high proportion of servile tenants recorded in the South West in 1086 may reflect the lasting impact of the loss of status suffered by the British under these arrangements.[21]

ANGLO-SAXON SETTLEMENT

If the Romans came to Exmoor largely in search of iron ore, what were the West Saxons looking for? Clearly the kings of Wessex wanted power and an enlarged territory. They also needed land with which to reward the men who had fought for them. However, we do not know how many West Saxons settled in the area and evidence of their material culture is hard to find, partly because few cemeteries can be associated with them. Such West-Saxon objects as have been found may simply have been acquired through trade by the indigenous British. Why, after all should a West-Saxon farmer abandon, say, the rich lowlands of Somerset to move to the wild hill country of Exmoor? While some young fighting men may have been ready to settle in the conquered land, it seems more likely that in general the principal beneficiaries were drawn from an absentee ruling élite. Having received large grants of land on Exmoor from the West-Saxon king, they probably sent men to oversee their new estates and collect the rents and renders from their new tenants and slaves. But if this was the case, we have to explain how the incomers retained control of the local inhabitants.[22]

Farming

The pattern of settlement on Anglo-Saxon Exmoor was determined by its dominant occupation: farming. There were no villages or market towns, only small hamlets. Settlement in southern Exmoor was widely dispersed and probably every valley site contained at least one farmstead. The British and incoming Anglo-Saxon farmers engaged predominantly in pastoral agriculture, but gradually farming on Exmoor changed and it was almost certainly the incomers who brought new practices. The old round buildings of the Iron Age gave way to rectangular ones, which offered greater flexibility, especially in the matter of size. Southern Exmoor's Anglo-Saxon farms would have been very small, their buildings barely intruding on the landscape. Trackways along the valleys and over the moors, groups of cattle and sheep, small buildings, and plumes of smoke from domestic fires and smithies would have been the main evidence of human activity in the area.

Studies of pollen deposits in the peats of Molland and other parishes on the fringe of Exmoor show that a form of mixed cultivation, not unlike that known in the 17th century as convertible husbandry, appeared on lower land in the eighth century. By the 11th century it had been extended to the Molland uplands and presumably to most of southern Exmoor where it continued to be practised until the area reverted to pasture in the late 16th and 17th centuries. It represented an extension of cultivated land, and its development in Exmoor in the early Middle Ages was perhaps driven by a growth in population, evidence that the local British inhabitants had not been driven out but remained there under their new West-Saxon lords.

This form of husbandry has been found in many upland areas alongside the open-field system practised in lowland England. Large enclosed 'infields' were used for cereal production, usually in alternate years. Fertility was maintained by grazing animals whose dung was ploughed in with the old grass before each cereal crop. Around these fields were areas of managed woodland, water meadow, 'outfields' and rough grazing. A single farming family would manage the infields, but co-operate with others to manage communal areas such as rough grazing. The 'outfields', taken from the moorland, were left under grass for up to eight years before being broken up for cereal crops and then laid back to grass.[23]

Arable cultivation was probably at its greatest extent on Exmoor in the late Anglo-Saxon period. Pollen analysis has shown that in the century before the Conquest high ground was broken for cereal crops. That level of arable farming was unsustainable, as is shown by the number of ploughteams on many estates by 1086. The important royal manor of Winsford had enough arable for 60 ploughs, but only 15 were recorded there. Even so, it contained a high quantity of arable for an Exmoor parish, perhaps needed to produce oats to feed the horses of its royal or comital lord. At

Exford, some ploughland had been laid to pasture, while in the area as a whole only two mills were recorded, one of them again at Winsford. It looks then as if settlement and crop production in southern Exmoor had already peaked in the late 11th century. The reasons for the decline are unknown and may be related to Exmoor's marginality, since in other areas the population continued growing until the early 14th century.[24]

The Forest Area

The one area of southern Exmoor where settlement appears to have been abandoned by the Anglo-Saxons was on the remote higher ground that formed the later forest. Marginal settlement was perhaps given up here, allowing wild animals to flourish. There is some evidence that grazing was abandoned in this area at the end of the Roman period with a resulting increase in heather. Such a regeneration of the natural flora may well have led to an increase in wild animals. That in turn would have made the upland areas desirable hunting grounds.[25]

THE LAND AND ITS DIVISIONS

The remoteness and marginality of Exmoor resulted in a complex governmental structure. The area lay in two shires, the boundaries of which may have been established relatively late on Exmoor itself. Manorial arrangements were also complicated by the existence of the West-Saxon forest area with its own officials.[26]

Shire and Hundred

The West-Saxon royal administration was based from a very early date on the shire, where the main royal representative, the ealdorman (later the sheriff), presided over the public court, collected the king's fines and dues, and led the shire forces into battle. Both the Exmoor shires appear to have been based upon British territories. Devon, with its shire centre at Exeter, is clearly based on eastern Dumnonia. Somerset derived its name from the large estate of Somerton, which included the former Roman town of Ilchester, arguably the Roman capital or *civitas* of the northern grouping of the Dumnonii's neighbours, the Durotriges from the third century AD.[27]

   The county boundary across Exmoor takes two forms. South of Sandyway in Exmoor parish the boundary follows natural watercourses. In the north it follows Hoccombe Water into Badgworthy Water to Cosgate or County Gate, then Coscombe

Figure 20 Litton Water, near Hawkridge, marking the ancient boundary between Devon and Somerset. From Sandyway the boundary follows Litton Water into Dane's Brook (Dunnock's brook in 1298) south to its junction with the river Barle, then an old road to the Den Brook, a tributary of the Exe.

to the sea. In the centre it is marked across the moors by barrows, standing stones, medieval boundary stones, and other features. This central section may date from 1207 when the Devon boundary was fixed under King John's agreement of 1204 to free Devon from forest law (see chapter 4).[28]

By the 10th century the hundred had emerged as a local administrative division of the shire with a court which might also be a manorial court. In 1086 Exmoor hundreds were small and may have been recent divisions of larger units. By then south Exmoor was divided among the hundreds of South Molton, Molland, Dulverton, Winsford, and Carhampton. There was a close relationship between hundreds, royal manors and churches. A royal manor needed officials to administer it and farmers and traders to supply it. It would, therefore, be a natural focus for the neighbourhood and a logical place on which to focus the hundred administration and the clergy. The hundreds of Dulverton and Winsford were centred on royal manors, which in Edward the Confessor's time had been granted to the Earls Harold and Tostig, sons of Earl Godwin and members of the greatest noble family in the England of their day. Godwin became earl of all Wessex in 1023, and as such was the principal royal official in Exmoor until his death in 1053, except for the brief period of his and his family's exile, 1051-2. He was succeeded as earl of Wessex by Harold, who was perhaps responsible for the allocation of Winsford to Tostig.

Manors and Estates

Southern Exmoor's estates, which may have their origins in the Romano-British period, were certainly well established before 1066. Landholding in the area, long dominated by the king, was still largely in the hands of his officials, the great earls, the leading members of the English élite. In the mid-11th century Dulverton and Molland (both held by Earl Harold), Winsford (held by Tostig) and North Molton (held by Edward the Confessor's queen, Edith) were all important manors, perhaps established on the edge of the forest because of the desirability of the area for hunting. Harold's and Tostig's holdings may represent lands traditionally assigned to the local ealdormen, and later to the earls of Wessex, in their capacity as royal officials. Although extensive, they had low tax assessments, either because they were beneficially rated or because the land was poor. Tostig's manor of Winsford included among its dependencies Withypool and Hawkridge, both places where the royal foresters of Exmoor had estates, and was perhaps the main focus of forest administration in the area.

Molland provides an example of the changes taking place in the mid-11th century. A royal manor, it gained in importance after it was granted to the all-powerful Harold Godwinson and became his principal holding in the area. By 1086 a hundred had also been based here, probably a recent creation through the division of South Molton hundred (with which it later re-merged). Molland's new importance was sustained when the manor passed to King William I. Its receipts included the earl's third penny, namely his share of the profits of justice derived from fines levied in the royal courts, in three neighbouring hundreds, including North Molton.

The main manors, kept in hand and managed by reeves, were Dulverton, Molland, and Winsford. They would have supplied produce for the royal household and money from the sale of marketable crops like grain and wool. Royal and non-royal manors had a demesne or home farm, worked by serfs assisted by the tenants for certain tasks, to provide the household with food. A demesne farm usually had enough arable to occupy up to three plough teams. The remainder of the manor was let to tenants who paid rents and dues and were also obliged to work on the lord's land for a number of days in the year.

Most non-royal manors were small in terms of 'hides', a unit of land that was probably enough to support one peasant household and usually assessed as 120 acres, but varied in size. They included several furlong or quarter-hide holdings in Exford and the land assessed at less than two hides shared by 13 thegns (lesser nobility) at Dulverton. The largest non-royal manor was Brushford, which was assessed at two hides with land for 12 ploughs and which before 1066 paid 24 sheep to the royal manor of Dulverton, possibly an ancient rent. Another, one of the Anstey manors, was held by Ednoth the Constable, a great landowner who was killed fighting against the sons of Earl Harold in 1068. Some of these small estates had surprisingly large populations, most notably Ashway and Hawkwell (both in Dulverton). Although the names now apply to single farmsteads and in the 11th century the two estates together were assessed at less than a hide, they contained a total of nine ploughlands, with woodland and extensive pasture in the north and west of the parish. How such small estates related to the larger royal manors is unknown.

The Anglo-Saxon Forest

Like the nearby royal forest of Dartmoor, Exmoor Forest may have originated in the ninth century; certainly, it was well-established by the mid-11th century when it was in the care of three royal foresters. It was probably under the Anglo-Saxon kings that local farmers established

Figure 21 A section from the Bayeux tapestry, in which Harold is seen hunting. Harold was a major landowner in southern Exmoor. *Reproduced by special permission of the City of Bayeux.*

grazing rights within the forest and local manors were granted the common pasture adjoining it. In 1066 the manors of Winsford and Almsworthy had substantial amounts of common pasture, probably Winsford Hill and Almsworthy Common, both outside the forest. The royal hunting ground was confined to the highest and most remote moors corresponding to the later Exmoor Forest but perhaps extending along the county boundary into Withypool and Hawkridge.[29]

In 1066 three royal foresters, Doda, Ælmer and Godric, held land in Withypool, presumably part of the rewards of office. Of thegnly status, they were liable for customary service to the reeve of Winsford, but owed him no dues. It is not clear why there were three and they may not have been of equal status. Probably Doda was the chief forester. He seems to have given his name to an enclosure of land in Withypool; Doda's hay, significantly, adjoins Woolpitland, named from the wolf pit which there, as in other Royal Forests, was used to trap wolves who preyed on deer and livestock. Doda held a neighbouring estate, probably Hawkridge but unnamed in the record, and may also have been the Doda who was lord of Stawe. This last estate, later known as Dodington, lay in the Quantocks, another Anglo-Saxon forest but one that did not survive into the later medieval period. It may have been given to Doda in exchange for Exmoor and perhaps he served there under the Norman royal forester.

The foresters' main responsibility was to ensure that the forest was properly managed, presumably by experienced local men. Anglo-Saxon forests do not appear to have been subject to the type of forest law imposed by the Normans, but settlement and farming would have been restricted to protect the royal game and those restrictions would have required regulation and enforcement in the local courts. The lands which the foresters held freely in return for these duties perhaps originated as clearings on the edge of the forest outside manorial jurisdiction. Situated between the established settlements on the royal estates of Dulverton and

Winsford and the forest itself, they probably comprised what, by the 17th century, were known as the 'free suitors' lands' in Withypool and Hawkridge. As in later times the foresters' estates came to be divided, their rights and duties seem to be vested in each new parcel of land, the occupiers of which were known as 'free suitors'. In 1086, however, this process had scarcely begun.[30]

The Parishes

Dumnonia was a Christian kingdom and missionaries from Wales and Ireland almost certainly reached the Exmoor coast in the sixth century. Inscribed standing stones at Winsford Hill and Culbone Hill are likely to be evidence of wealthy Christians in the area. Cynegils, king of Wessex, converted to Christianity in 635, and so West Saxons who moved into Exmoor thereafter are likely to have been Christians.

The parish structure emerged later. In the early Anglo-Saxon period the countryside in many places was served by minsters, communities of priests who travelled the area preaching and celebrating the sacraments. They often enjoyed royal patronage and were usually situated in areas of good cultivable land, which would support the clergy; from the eighth century they were increasingly associated with large burial grounds. By the ninth century there were minsters at Braunton, Exeter and Taunton and by the 11th at South Molton and Carhampton. Carhampton probably served northern Exmoor; its links with

Figure 22 The excavation of the Caratacus stone, Winsford, 1937. E.T. MacDermot is seen on the left and H. St George Grey on the right. Thought to be a British Christian monument, the stone is inscribed CARAACI NEPUS, usually interpreted as kinsman of Caratacus, the first-century British rebel against Roman rule. The excavation found no burial.

the area are evident from the customary renders of sheep made
to the royal manor by the coastal estates of Oare and Allerford
before 1066. Given the terrain and the distances involved, it is
however unlikely that Carhampton could have served estates
south of the forest. South Molton, with its four landholding
priests, probably served south-west Exmoor. It has been suggested
that because it has a circular churchyard, like Carhampton and
other early church sites, Dulverton church may have been in
existence in the early Anglo-Saxon period. As a royal manor and
hundred, Dulverton would have been well-placed to serve as an
ecclesiastical centre for south-east Exmoor.[31]

Landowners wanted their own church, partly for status and
convenience and partly as a way of holding the community of
tenants together. The territory which a local church served – the
parish – is likely often to have coincided with the founder's local
holdings and to have been stabilised by the customary dues
contributed by, or exacted from, the lord's tenants for its support.
The custom of holding baptisms in the church itself, and burials
in the churchyard, helped the lord to maintain control over the
families of his tenants and slaves. The parishes of southern Exmoor
were focused upon the main manors whose lords, like Robert of
Auberville at Hawkridge and Mauger of Cartrai, tenant of the
count of Mortain at Brushford, probably endowed churches and
priests. Surviving Norman work suggests that on Exmoor the local
parish church was an established feature by the late 11th century,
although only landholding minsters like South Molton were
recorded in Domesday Book.

The emergence of the parish was a prolonged process, but
appears to have taken place on Exmoor in the 11th century. To the
north of Exmoor the parish boundary of Culbone was marked
out in the mid-Anglo-Saxon period when crosses were placed
on prehistoric stones. No similar boundary marks have been
found in southern Exmoor but it is possible that early churches
like Dulverton had a defined parish before the 11th century.
Since parish boundaries were largely determined by units of
landownership, they were not necessarily dictated by natural
features, and indeed on Exmoor such features are not important,
except at Dulverton whose eastern and western boundaries are
largely marked by the rivers Exe and Barle.[32]

Exmoor parishes are generally large. That reflects both the size
of the estates which they were founded to serve and – since they
had no landed endowment – the need for sufficient customary
dues (especially tithes) for their staffing and maintenance.
Powerful lords, such as the king and the earls could enforce
support for their church throughout their manor. That

Norman Craftsmanship

Christianity, although well established on Exmoor during the Anglo-Saxon period, has left few physical remains and little evidence of pre-Conquest churches. Part of an Anglo-Saxon cross survives at Porlock, to the north of the study area, whilst Culbone church's simple two-cell plan and possible 11th-century window suggest pre-Norman origins. The early herringbone work at Exton is not easily datable although it, too, suggests the church is among Exmoor's oldest. After the Conquest, there seems to have been much more activity as the parish structure emerged on Exmoor. Although extensive restoration of parish churches in the 19th and 20th centuries has often destroyed or masked early medieval fabric, evidence of post-conquest church building can be found in surviving furnishings. In southern Exmoor seven churches have Norman fonts, a remarkable survival in a relatively small area which may mark the date at which those churches were founded or acquired parochial responsibilities such as baptism.

In general, settlements now cluster around most churches, although Exford stands isolated from the village beside an important axial route across the hills, now the B3224. At Winsford the church was probably built next to the manor house, as is customary in lowland areas. In the Ansteys the two churches were built next to the chief houses of two manors, although at East Anstey not by the most important, whose chapel did not become a parish church. Given the concentration of large estates, it was likely to have been the king or wealthy nobles who built the churches. A great deal of expense would have been incurred not only on the building but also in providing fonts, altars, linen, embroidered vestments, candlesticks, and crosses.

Churches were probably the only substantial stone buildings on Exmoor and would have dominated the landscape. That the origins of churches were important to parishioners is shown in the common practice of preserving Norman south doorways during later rebuilding. At Hawkridge the fine Romanesque doorway indicates that the church was built during this period and at considerable expense. The neighbouring villages of Winsford and Exton have a re-set Norman inner door and a Norman nave respectively, as does the church of St Mary at Molland.

Figure A *Winsford font. The Norman fonts at Brushford, Hawkridge, Molland, Twitchen, West Anstey, Winsford, and Withypool vary in shape and design. They were carved from large blocks of stone and most carry cable or chevron patterns. The square ones may be later but the precise sequence is unknown.*

Figure B *Molland's square font has a scalloped edging. Brushford font is also square, but of Purbeck marble, now mounted on a modern cluster of columns. It was possibly given by the de Cartrai family, Domesday tenants of the manor.*

Figure 23 Map of parishes, churches and numbers of Domesday households in southern Exmoor. Domesday estates did not coincide with parish boundaries. The population figure for Twitchen, part of which lay in North Molton manor, has been estimated from later medieval references.

presumably explains the large size of Dulverton and Winsford, the area's largest parishes, each covering over 8,000 acres. Lords with powerful tenants might have to adopt a more voluntary approach, or limit the area where maintenance was enforced. In Anstey, an area divided between four small manors, two parishes were eventually established and at Exford eight estates came together to support one church. On smaller estates the lord may have had a chapel, as in Dunster, but his people owed their attendance and tithes to the parish church.[33]

The original dedications of most Exmoor churches are unknown, but there is some evidence that the people of Exmoor continued to revere the memory of the early saints who brought Christianity to the area. West Anstey church is dedicated to the

Cornish saint, Petroc, whose cult centre, originally at Padstow, had by the 11th century been transferred to Bodmin in Cornwall and who was also dedicatee of 19 churches in the South West. In 1086 the bishop of Coutances held estates in Anstey and Molland and interest in the saint may have spread from there to his see-city. Interestingly, Walter of Coutances, archbishop of Rouen and English justiciar (principal officer of state) in the late 12th century, gave a reliquary to hold Petroc's relics in Bodmin. Exford's supposed former dedication to St Salvyn may indicate early origins, but nothing is known of the saint.[34]

THE ORDERING OF LATE ANGLO-SAXON SOCIETY

Figure 24 Downscombe Farm, probably on the site of the farmstead at the heart of the small manor of Downscombe, held by a woman called Æthelgifu in 1086.

Anglo-Saxon society, in Exmoor as elsewhere, was hierarchical, divided into noble, free and unfree classes, with numerous slaves. No important noble resided in the area, although as we have seen, some, such as Earl Harold or Ednoth the Constable, held land there in the mid-11th century. Lesser thegnly landholders in the area in 1066, also possibly non-resident, included Ulf, who held less than two virgates at Hawkwell, but who may also have held Woolston in Stogursey and Idstock in Cannington. A virgate was about

Figure 25 Anglo-Saxon ploughing and sowing, as shown in the Bayeux tapestry. Many agricultural workers on large estates would have been slaves. In Devon and on royal estates there were usually three or four serfs to each plough on the demesne; in Somerset there were two. *Reproduced by special permission of the City of Bayeux.*

thirty acres, although it may have been more on Exmoor. Another thegn, Ordwulf, held two hides at Brushford in 1066 and may also have owned manors in Devon, several of which, like Brushford, passed to the count of Mortain. In general, the peak of resident local society was represented by modest landholders, such as the 13 thegns at Dulverton or perhaps by the Royal Foresters. A few survived the Conquest, including Ulf, and his co-tenant Wulmer, Ednoth (not the Constable) and a woman, Æthelgifu.

There were probably many freehold farmers in southern Exmoor. Bicca, Brant, and Hringa, who gave their names to Bickingcott and Praunsley in Twitchen, and Ringcombe in West Anstey, may have been freeholders who carved out new farms beyond the established estates. Some of these farms, such as Bickingcott, remained freeholds.[35]

The peasant farmers, or *villani*, were higher in status than their medieval successors, the villeins, but were required to do labour service on their landlord's farm. These obligations tied a villein to the land because if he went away and left his service unperformed he would forfeit his farm, which he held of his lord. They formed the largest group in the population of southern Exmoor.

Smallholders, also known as bordars, formed a third of the population of southern Exmoor in 1086. In Withypool and Exford there were more bordars than *villani*. Their holdings may have been too small to support a family and they probably supplemented their incomes by working as part-time labourers for others. The bordars of Withypool may have been employed as woodsmen, herdsmen, and huntsmen by the Royal Foresters. Bordars may have included craftspeople, rarely mentioned in the Domesday survey; smiths, carpenters, masons, shoemakers, and others would have needed a smallholding. The only specialist occupation recorded in the area of southern Exmoor was the pigman at Anstey but, just outside, North Molton manor (which then included Twitchen) had four ironworkers and 15 pigmen. Nothing is known about the location of the bordars' holdings.[36]

In 1086 there were as many as 70 households of *servi* (the Latin word for slave) in southern Exmoor. By the mid-11th century this term was applied both to personal and household slaves (not recorded in the survey) and to 'serfs'; agricultural workers bound to labour on their owner's land. Slaves were numerous in Anglo-Saxon society. A criminal, a family that could not pay compensation owed for a wrong to another family, a pauper, or a captive in war might be enslaved for a time, or until 'manumitted' (set free). As the child of a slave was born unfree, the south-western counties had large numbers of slaves and serfs, especially on the royal estates, although many small estates had none. Somerset manors usually had two serfs, but Devon three or four, as every demesne ploughteam needed two men to guide an eight-oxen team and its plough. The four small Anstey manors had a total of 19 serfs. The labour of the wives and children of serfs would also be owed to their lord. Tasks such as herding stock, making cheese, spinning and weaving, sewing, washing, and cleaning would probably be given to the members of servile families.[37]

After the Norman Conquest slavery declined in its Anglo-Saxon form and serfdom became confined to the families of tenants who were legally unfree but lived and worked on their own holdings. Landowners probably preferred to depend on labour services and wage labour rather than keep serfs who had to be fed and housed with their families all the year round whether they worked or not.

AFTER 1086

After the Conquest, the royal and comital manors of southern Exmoor passed to King William I while other estates were given to his followers and to senior churchmen. In Devon, Baldwin the sheriff and Hugh of Avranches, earl of Chester and William's nephew, were given estates at Anstey and Molland; in Somerset, Robert, count of Mortain, William's half-brother, received Brushford, Robert of Auberville (or Odburville) obtained Hawkridge and Withypool, and Roger of Courcelles and William of Mohun divided many estates between them, including those at Exford.

None of the new owners of manors lived on Exmoor, although William de Mohun lived close by at Dunster. From the local perspective perhaps the most significant newcomer was Robert of Auberville, William I's leading serjeant in Somerset and almost certainly the royal forester, the first of successive officers responsible for enforcing Norman forest law.[38]

Among the minor landholders were a handful of Normans like William who held Broford in Dulverton, and the Breton Ruald Adobed who held Pulham and Praunsley but even they probably did not live on those estates. Most of the recorded tenants and sub-tenants were English and unless the king or his followers came hunting or a landowner came to hold a

Figure 26 Penny of William I struck at Watchet. By 1066 southern Exmoor was dominated by 'Terra Regis' (king's land), which was transferred to King William or given to his followers and to churchmen.

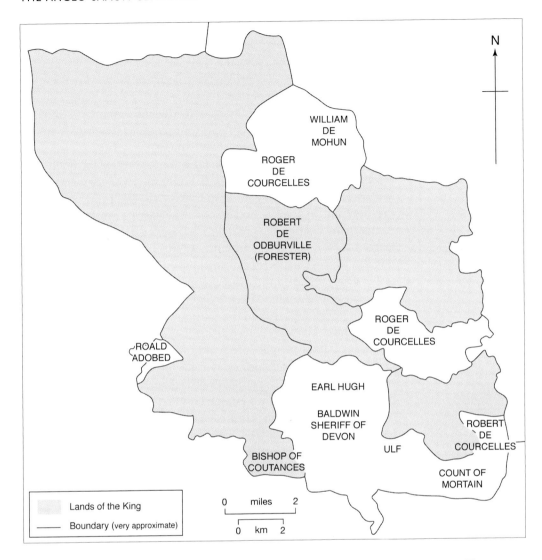

Figure 27 Landowners of southern Exmoor in 1086. The boundaries are very approximate. None of the lords and bishops lived on Exmoor.

court few Normans would have been seen on Exmoor. For most of the population life would have continued after 1066 as it had before. They paid their rents to a different landlord and would eventually adapt to a system of manorial administration dependent on written records.[39]

Because of the Domesday survey we know a great deal about the agricultural estates of southern Exmoor. A good example is Almsworthy, an estate which probably covered the north-west of Exford parish including the valleys of the Allcombe, Greenland and Swincombe waters. Originally held by the Anglo-Saxon Edric, by 1086 it was in the hands of Roger of Courcelles. Roger would have installed a reeve, a manorial official, or a tenant farmer to run the estate, which would have been divided between his home farm (his demesne) and the tenanted land. Although Almsworthy had no taxable value in 1086 and still had the very low assessment of a virgate (a quarter of a hide), it was recorded as having cultivated land for six ploughs. A considerable amount of arable, since a ploughland was the amount of land an eight-oxen ploughteam could cultivate in a season. At Almsworthy, some may have been uncultivated, since there were only four ploughteams, but even so it was clearly a highly beneficial assessment.

In all, in addition to the home farm, Roger's estate included six farmsteads and nine smallholdings. His home farm comprised arable worked by a ploughteam and two serfs, eight acres of meadow and 30 acres of underwood. The pasture, probably Almsworthy Common, would have been grazed not only by Roger's eight oxen, horse, six cattle, 47 sheep, and 27 nanny goats, but also by the tenants' stock, which is not listed, except for the 24 oxen, which made up their three ploughteams. The goats, who as browsers would not have been welcome in the woodland, may have been supported by scrub in the valleys.[40]

The Domesday survey recorded heads of households but omits all kinds of other people. It tells us nothing, for example, about family members or servants or about non-landholding clergy, craftsmen, and landless paupers. Some estates, such as Doda's holding, one of the Exford estates, and Pixton in Dulverton, have no recorded population. Estimates of average household size are usually given as four or five; allowing for missing households and for large manorial complexes such as Winsford or Molland, we might use the upper figure for southern Exmoor. That indicates a total population of perhaps 1,780, excluding lords and their households. The density of population was lower than on the lowlands, but at least a third of the area was uninhabited forest and moor. Dulverton, Molland, and Winsford had the largest populations but no evidence of urban functions. Withypool's population appears to have been similar to that of 1801, reflecting substantial settlement by 1086.[41]

People would have lived in hamlets as well as isolated farmsteads and there must have been centres of population on the royal estates. Cultivating land with teams of oxen required farms to be grouped together, as few farmers on Exmoor could afford or accommodate the eight oxen required for a ploughteam and the Domesday survey implied that such ploughteams were shared by tenant farmers. Two villein tenants in West Anstey had half a ploughteam, possibly on the farms now known as East and West Ringcombe, which they may have combined with that of a close neighbour such as the farmer of Brimblecombe in Molland. At Broford in Dulverton, described as a hamlet in 1298, four farmers shared a ploughteam. Exmoor hamlets were usually dispersed along a lane like West, Middle, and East Lee in Molland, each with its own enclosed fields.

By the 11th century settlement on Exmoor had probably reached its greatest extent. Only the forest was clear of habitation, apart from Badgworthy on its northern edge, and that was abandoned before the end of the Middle Ages apart from a cottage. Sources for Molland, North Molton and other manors in Devon indicate that there was little change in settlement between the 11th and 13th centuries although the lowland population of England as a whole trebled between 1086 and 1300. Until the forest was enclosed in the 19th century there may have been no significant increase in the number of Exmoor settlements.[42]

Chapter 4

The Middle Ages

Figure 28 The 14th-century cross in Withypool churchyard, a community focus.

In the century following the Norman Conquest two major changes impacted on the community of southern Exmoor. First, the extension of Norman forest law over most of Exmoor from Dulverton to the coast restricted the activities of local people used to exploiting the wild resources of the moor. While this represented a tightening of the royal grip on the forest, the royal estates were largely transferred to the nobility and the church and some Domesday manors were divided. The manor and the church increasingly governed the everyday lives of the people of southern Exmoor. The second major change was that local people came to feel an allegiance to the parish where they were born, lived, had their children baptised, and where their families were buried.

THE ROYAL FOREST

In the late 12th century Exmoor Forest may have extended south from the sea to the Devon river Yeo, and from the rivers Bray and Haddon in the west, to the Exe and Horner Water on the east. The term 'forest' in medieval England did not refer to woodland but to a legal sanctuary for game animals preserved for the sport or table of the king. Lowland forests like the New Forest were more wooded but trees do not grow so well on uplands such as Exmoor. Jurisdiction varied from the complete implementation of forest law to a simple ban on hunting deer. It may be that for outlying Exmoor parishes only the latter applied.

The inclusion of estates, farms and villages changed the nature of the forest in the 12th and 13th centuries; in 1184 a collection of laws called the Assize of the Forest, subjected people to forest law in their own homes. The laws were designed to protect the 'vert' (woodland and vegetation), deer, wild boar, and other animals for hunting, and meant that people were forbidden to take game, cut trees, collect fuel, cut turf, clear or cultivate land, or graze livestock without payment. Farmers could not assart (extend their cultivated land by clearing and improving new land), and there were restrictions on the dogs and weapons they could keep. New settlement was impossible without breaking the law.

The way in which the laws were enforced could sometimes stir resentment. The office of Royal Forester or warden, probably established in the late 11th century, was a hereditary post held by

N

Bristol   Channel

Lynmouth
Bay

*Porlock
Bay*

COUNTISBURY

CULBONE

Bossington

MARTINHOE

PORLOCK

LYNTON

BRENDON

OARE

LUCCOMBE

PARRACOMBE

STOKE
PERO

Part of
Wootton
Courtney

CHALLACOMBE

Harwood

EXMOOR
FOREST

CUTCOMBE

EXFORD

S O M E R S E T

HIGH
BRAY

WINSFORD

WITHYPOOL

CHARLES

EXTON

NORTH
MOLTON

HAWKRIDGE

TWITCHEN

EAST
BUCKLAND

MOLLAND

WEST
ANSTEY

DULVERTON

D E V O N

BISHOP'S
NYMPTON

EAST
ANSTEY

Boundaries of parishes wholly
or partly in forest *c.* 1200

County boundary

Study area outside forest

Approximate extent
of forest 1219

Approximate extent
of forest 1300

0   miles   10

0   km   10

Figure 29 The changing
boundaries of Exmoor
Forest 1200–1300.

the lords of Newton Plecy in North Petherton. Under-foresters
like Walter and Robert, who witnessed a grant to Forde Abbey in
the early 13th century, are likely to have bought their appointment
from the forester and until 1298 had to make their living from
imposing charges on the local people. In 1276 the jurors of
Brushford manor, which lay outside the forest, complained that

> John de Camera, a forester of Exmore, charged William of la
> Worthe concerning a certain stag he was thought to have taken
> from the … Forest … and imprisoned him until he had from
> him twenty shillings. And afterwards the country came and
> acquitted the said William of la Worthe.

Figure 30   Red deer hinds, young male and stag on Exmoor. Edward II sent his huntsmen to Exmoor to kill 20 stags in 1315 but that is the only such record. Exmoor was too remote to interest kings with access to forests closer to home.

By the 13th century the administration of forest law was carried out by two Exmoor verderers, judicial officers answerable directly to the king and elected in the county court. They were unpaid but held forest courts, kept records of offences to present to the king's court, and held inquiries into deaths of deer. There were also 12 regarders, who were required to inspect the forest every three years, and woodwards, who were appointed by the owners of woodland within the forest, and did most of the work on the ground, catching poachers and finding dead deer or damage to the land.[43]

Breaking the Law Somerset fared worse than Devon with regard to forest law. Devon's Exmoor was disafforested (freed from forest law) in 1204, by a charter costing 1,000 marks (£666), and Dartmoor was disafforested in 1240, when pioneer farms were created there. But in Somerset, attempts to disafforest Dulverton, Exton, and Winsford in 1219 were unsuccessful, despite the fact that in 1204 Forde Abbey had obtained from King John freedom from most forest jurisdiction over its estates including Ashway in Dulverton. In the 1240s, the jurors of Carhampton hundred complained that the forester took the herbage of their common pasture but their case was dismissed.

An itinerant Royal Forest court called the eyre dealt with those accused of unlawful hunting or making assarts. On 26 November 1257 it was held at Ilchester, some 50 miles from Exmoor, and a long journey in early winter. In Hawkridge, Elias of la Sele (Zeal) and seven others were fined for sowing assarts. The rector was charged 10s. for having grown winter and spring corn on a four-acre assart and 3s. for sowing a new one-and-a-half-acre assart. The fine was probably greatly in excess of the value of his crops and he had to forfeit the new assart to the king.

The record of the court of May 1270, also in Ilchester, illustrates the increasing pressure on the forest as an exclusive royal hunting ground. In 1257 a few people had ignored the law and hunted in the forest, and they had fled when noticed, but in 1270 many more incidents of illegal hunting were recorded. Some of these incidents dated back 10 years, and some of the suspects had died, but several others were imprisoned. Most offenders, some of whom were gentlemen and clergy, came from within the forest, but others came from Bampton, Lynton, and North Molton. The rector of Oare was fined 20s. for receiving venison at the parsonage from his son and servant, and Thomas de Tracy, who was hunting in Devon in 1266, was caught at Hawkridge and taken to Tawstock after his stag ran into the forest. Thomas le Shetere of Gourt and William Wyme of Bremley from Molland entered the forest in 1267,

> with bows and arrows with intent to do evil to the venison of the Lord King, and shot one hind and afterwards chased her into the wood at Langcombe outside the boundaries of the forest and there took her and carried her away to their houses in Molland, … they were harboured in the house of John then the chaplain of Hawkridge, who consented to their evil deeds. The same chaplain came and is detained in prison. And the others have not come …

The sheriff of Devon was required to bring them to court; Dulverton, Ashway Ashwick, and Hurdecombe townships were fined, but the chaplain was pardoned for the sake of the king's soul. The court also fined seven men from Exford and Withypool for cutting peat in the king's demesne, but the Royal Forester was accused of failing to raise the alarm when poachers from Anstey had been hunting for three days.[44]

For local people it was the restrictions on farming and fuel gathering that caused most trouble. In 1279 a list of grievances included the following complaint:

> … the men who work in their waste ground to make enclosures to sow corn, although the king has no demesne, the foresters arrest these to come before them, and say that they have made waste and illegal enclosure, if they do not their will to have peace; and from each man holding land they claim to have the skin of a lamb or a halfpenny, and say that it is their fee.[45]

Perambulations of the forest in 1298 and 1300 boldly stated that the manors and parishes lay outside the forest and had been wrongfully included. That was confirmed in 1301 but it took several years for the forest officials to accept the new boundaries and allow assarting and swaling (controlled burning of the moors to improve grazing, an ancient custom practised in many English uplands). Poaching continued to be severely punished; James Audley was presented in 1364 for having his park in North Molton so badly enclosed that the king's deer could get in and, by inference, remain.[46]

Free Suitors The estates of the 11th-century foresters in Hawkridge and Withypool had probably been allocated with their duties and privileges by the Crown or the Royal Forester. Until the 19th century these lands, including Dodhays and Woolpitland which were names associated with the early forest, carried with them 52 'suits' (rights and obligations) whose holders were known as 'free suitors'. That term first appears in the 17th century but they were probably the freeholders recorded in the mid-13th century, many of whom bore the names of later 'free suit' lands. The lands, first named in 1797, were incorporated into farms. The original basis on which suits were allocated is unknown but they were divided or accumulated with the lands to which they belonged. As well as doing suit to the forest courts, free suitors attended the 'drift' of the forest. This meant riding around on horseback rounding up the ponies, cattle and sheep, and driving them back to the pound. They also had to patrol the forest and serve on a coroner's jury if a corpse was found in the forest. In return, for each suit they held, they had free grazing in the forest for 140 sheep, five horses, as many cattle as could be wintered on the land to which the suit was attached, and until the 17th century a sow and a number of young pigs, depending on their age. They could take as much turf, heath, and fern as they could consume on their holdings and fish in the rivers in the forest and in the lands to which the suits were attached. The 'suitors at large', everyone else who owed suit to the forest court, including the owners of other land in Hawkridge and Withypool had to pay for grazing.

Local forest courts, which brought together representatives of all the communities of greater Exmoor from both sides of the county boundary, and manor courts efficiently maintained this system. The bailiff and four or five tenants from each manor attended the forest court on a rotational basis. It was an opportunity to do business and gather news, and each manor had its own branding iron so that the ownership of the animals

Forest and Manor Courts

Figure A   *Medieval Lanacre bridge, Withypool, near the meeting place of the forest court, probably on land later called Court Hams. The early courts would have been social and business meetings at the end of the long upland winter.*

Forest Courts

In much of England in the Middle Ages, routine business relating to local communities was conducted at the appropriate manorial court before the lord of the manor or his representative. Serious crimes were generally dealt with by royal officials – either the sheriff or a royal justice at the shire and hundred courts (although in many cases manor courts might also function as hundred courts). A major exception were those areas that were under forest law, which imposed a wide range of exceptional fines and penalties and were operated through special courts with their own officials.

Forest and manorial courts had a long life, but from the 16th century onwards were of increasingly minor importance. Most had disappeared by the 19th century.

Forest law was largely implemented through royal itinerant courts called 'eyres', but local forest courts

known as the 'swainmote' or 'swanimote courts' were
held twice a year in the spring. The first was held near
Lanacre Bridge in Withypool. The second opened
in Hawkridge churchyard, but by the 17th century
adjourned to Withypool, possibly to the alehouse. There
are no medieval swainmote records, but it would have
punished people for entering the forest with a gun, bow,
or dog or for illegal fishing or grazing. In the 18th century
courts moved to Simonsbath and by 1807 only one
annual court was held for collecting the chief rents and
enjoying a good dinner. The last court was held in 1818.

Manor Courts

There are few records of the Exmoor manors, but their
owners would have kept courts once or twice a year,
large manors more often. The court baron dealt with
tenancies and the court leet with community business
such as nuisances and disputes. The homage, or jury, was
drawn from the leading tenants to present offences and
declare manorial customs, which also applied to the lord or
lady. Then custom was binding in law for the lords of the
manor as well as for the tenents; the latter, for example,
could demand their lords carry out duties such as repairing
the pound. Constables to keep the peace, haywards to
manage the fields, and tithingmen were usually elected at
the autumn court. Records of proceedings were entered
on parchment and new tenants would have a copy of
the entry relating to their tenancy. Manorial tenancy was
therefore known as copyhold.

Court records usually start with the date and
the name of the lord or the steward. Then come the
essoins (excuses) made by people for not attending.
Other defaulters were amerced (fined). Business

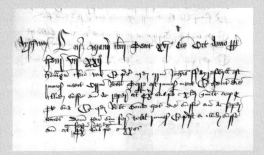

Figure B   *Court record for Ashway in Dulverton held on
16 October 1506, from a draft court book covering many
manors. John Fayreswyll and Robert Torre needed to do
some roof repairs and Robert Bonde was ordered to repair
all his buildings, which were ruinous, or pay 20s.*

included changes of tenancy, payment of heriots (an
animal or money due to the lord after a tenant died),
and cases between tenants. The jury or officers would
present offences such as straying animals, houses in
need of repair, pollution or diversion of watercourses,
selling ale at excessive prices, or selling bad meat.

In November 1322 a Dulverton court dealt with
damage to crops by livestock and illegal felling. The elder
William of Draydon lost his office of woodward for felling
an oak without licence and Stephen atte Mershe was
sworn in his place. Nicholas atte Hole, charcoal burner,
had cut down an oak beyond his boundary.

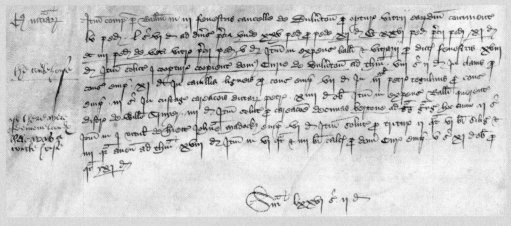

Figure C   *Extract from Dulverton manor account, 1425-6, detailing expenses of installing chancel windows and tiling
the court house. Courts produced an income for the landowner such as Taunton Priory, which received £4 18s. 2d. from its
Dulverton courts in 1425-6.*

Figure 31 Seal of Hugh
de Turberville, lord of
Dulverton, on a late 12th-
or early 13th-century
deed of land at Hele and
Pixton in Dulverton.

grazing in the forest could be identified. Without payments for grazing it is difficult to see how the Crown could have afforded to maintain the forest.[47]

THE MEDIEVAL MANOR

In the century after the Norman Conquest the royal estate on Exmoor was broken up and granted away; other large estates such as that of Roger de Courcelles experienced similar changes. Many owners gave estates to followers, retaining only a minimal overlordship such as the right to call for the service of knights in time of war, and some gave land to endow religious houses.

In Somerset, where the restrictions of forest law may have discouraged some landowners from living on Exmoor, manors were often in the hands of absentees. This was the case in Dulverton. It was no longer a royal manor, but remained the centre of a hundred and it was held by the absentee Robert de Schete of Combe. However, in about 1254 Roger de Reigny won possession of the manor, while de Schete kept the hundred because he had held the court. This decision was unpopular with Justice Henry de Bracton because manor and hundred had always been held together.

The most obvious absentee owners in Somerset were religious houses. The Augustinian canons of Taunton Priory had acquired Dulverton church and its land by 1155, and by 1337 they owned

Figure 32 Edbrooke
House and farm,
Winsford, in the late 19th
century. The river Exe
is behind the house and
the small building to the
left stood on Edbrooke
bridge. The brook runs
from the lower right
under the L-shaped
building. Both the house
and bridge are medieval
in origin.

Figure 33 A 13th-century coffin lid at Hawkridge inscribed with the name William, said to be William de Plecy (*d.*1274). Hawkridge was one of his manors and he may have had a house there.

virtually the whole of Dulverton manor, but sold part of Ashway to Forde Abbey (Devon, now Dorset). The Cistercian monks of Neath Abbey had bought the southern half of Exford by the 1190s; well known for their prowess in sheep farming, they had contemplated moving there, but are not thought to have done so. The tithes (a tax or levy usually paid to the church) of the Mohun estate in Exford were given to Dunster priory in the 13th century, while Wilton Abbey held land in Withypool, and Barlynch Priory had property in Winsford. Taunton Priory let its demesne farm at Dulverton and collected rents and tithes, kept courts and paid for repairs.[48]

Exford was consolidated by the late 12th century into two principal manors of Almsworthy and Exford. By contrast Hawkridge, Withypool and Brushford were divided among many owners by the end of the 14th century. Ancient freehold estates, like the Sanford family's estate of Edbrooke and the Incledon property at Bradley, both in Winsford, were sometimes regarded as manors by their, usually resident, owners.

Among possible resident landowners in the early 14th century were the Ives family of Brushford and the Bluetts at Almsworthy, although there is no record of a manor house on either estate and no church monuments. Richard Durant and John Heyron, who both held shares in the manors of Exton, Hawkridge and Withypool, appear to have lived on Exmoor in 1327 and, at Dulverton, landowners Hawise de Pyne and Richard of Hawkwell were resident. By 1330, however, the house of Hawise, owner of half Dulverton manor, was apparently unoccupied again.[49]

By contrast, the Devon manors, perhaps due to their early freedom from forest jurisdiction, had owners who were often resident and able to increase the size of their estates. Thus, the former hundredal manor of North Molton had expanded by the 13th century to include Pulham, and probably Praunsley, in Twitchen, while Molland had incorporated Wadham in Knowstone parish to the south. Molland was particularly important, as is shown by the fact that William de Wadham and Roger de Whitefield paid more tax than their overlord William de Botreaux in 1332. The Zouches and the Botreauxs both developed fortified manor places and parks, probably in the second half of the 13th century, and by the same period the Anstey manors had taken their names from the families of Reigny and Moyne (Money) in West Anstey, and from Crewes in East Anstey. These were later divided into numerous shares. Richard Reigny of West Anstey appears to have been a wealthy man judging by the large sums of money owing to him in 1307-8.

MEDIEVAL SETTLEMENTS AND FARMS

The hamlets and farmsteads of medieval Exmoor were gathered into parish communities and 'tithings', a medieval unit of jurisdiction that accounted for a tenth of a hundred. Society was structured in such a way that people would come together to attend church and court and assist each other in need. But they did not always do this lawfully. Almsworthy, for example, appears to have been a hideout for thieves. In the 1240s, Ralph of Riscombe fled and was outlawed for harbouring three thieves including an Irishman and the tithing was also fined because one of its members was responsible for a suspect in custody who escaped. On another occasion two Almsworthy men gave security for William of Exford to appear at the assizes to answer for treasure he had found, but he failed to appear.[50]

Medieval hamlets included Ashway in Dulverton, recorded in 1257; Highercombe in Dulverton, recorded in 1270; Brightworthy and Lanacre in Withypool; Edbrooke in Winsford; and Broford, Hawkwell, Liscombe, Marsh, and Old Shute in Dulverton, recorded in 1298. Farms in those hamlets may have been small like the five tenements that made up Lyshwell hamlet in the early 19th century, each with between two and five infields of varying size around the houses. Separated from the rest of Molland parish by large areas of common, this small settlement, now a single farm, adjoined Cloggs in Hawkridge and was possibly responsible for signs of cultivation on Molland moor.[51]

Farms and Farmers

Given the high density of farmsteads in the 11th century, the lack of new land to be exploited, and the reluctance of the Crown or other lords to release demesne land, any population pressure could only be accommodated by dividing farms. That may account for pairs of farms such as East and West Nethercote in Winsford, presumably the farms of Adam and William of Nethercote in 1270, North and South Ley in Exford, Higher and Lower Chilcott in Dulverton, and East and West Gatcombe in Molland. Sowerhill in Brushford was two farms by 1327 when the occupiers were among the highest taxpayers in the parish. The process of new farm creation may have continued after the Middle Ages but few farms were named after families as is common in lowland areas. King's Farm in Withypool is a rare exception.

In Molland, conventionary tenure, as used in Devon and Cornwall, may have affected farming. Conventionary tenants held

Figure 34 Bungsland, East Anstey, a medieval longhouse remodelled in the late 16th or early 17th century when a shippon was added. The longhouse, with humans and animals under one roof and originally with a single entrance for people and livestock, was common in the uplands of south-west England.

short leases, usually seven years, secured by the highest bidder. That deterred long-term family interest and may have been a disincentive to investing in improvement. The manorial extents – descriptions and valuations of all the items on the manor – of Molland show a shift from villein to conventionary tenure between 1274 and 1302, when 26 *conventionarii* each held half a virgate, around fifteen acres.[52]

The surviving medieval records for southern Exmoor are rich in farm names. Some 65 were recorded during the 13th and early 14th centuries. A few later disappeared from the record, including Everadiston in Dulverton recorded in about 1200. Its lands lay amongst those of Pixton and it may have been absorbed into that estate. The same deed recorded Hinam, Ashway, and Steart, also in Dulverton. The records of the assizes (circuit judges) mention Bommertown in Molland in 1238, Riscombe in Exford and Blackford in Winsford in 1242-3, and Bremley and Smallacombe in Molland, Cherricombe in East Anstey, Hill in West Anstey, and Bickingcott in Twitchen in 1244. In 1270 the forest eyre fined Roger le Erceveske of Ashweie, Richard of la Slade, Baldwin of Hindeham (Hinam), Baldwin of Loscumbe (Liscombe), Robert of Wolweye, William of Stocham, Robert and Thomas of la Hele, all of Dulverton, and William of Upcote, William of Nethercote, William of Blakeford, and William of Cnaploc, all of Winsford, for failing to attend.[53]

Inquisitions *post mortem* (royal enquiries into the estates of deceased landowners) provide a further source for farms. Among

the jurors giving evidence in 1274 about the estates of Reginald
Botreaux were William de Polamesford, John de Smalcombe,
Simon de Bremelcumb, Robert de Gopweill, and Richard de
Lystelhele, from Molland farms still traceable as Pulham or
Pulsworthy, Smallacombe, Brimblecombe, Guphill, and Lyshwell.
The lay subsidies of the early 14th century also provide evidence
of place names, as many people were still known by their place of
origin or residence.[54]

Arable Cultivation

Many Exmoor farmsteads would have been barely accessible in
bad weather. Farmers needed to be self sufficient in providing food
for themselves and their animals, which meant cultivating arable
crops despite the poor quality of the soil. Pressure to produce crops
was such that hill land was ploughed on Winsford Hill, south of
Lanacre in Withypool, and in 1257 illegal assarts and enclosures
in the forest amounting to 24½ acres were sown mostly with
spring and winter corn, rye, and oats. For the same reason, in
1400, tenants Richard Kyng and his wife, Gonilde, were allowed to
plough meadow in East Anstey provided that it was restored after
a reasonable time. Any grain produced had to be ground at their
lord's mill.[55]

    Pollen analysis of the moors shows that arable cultivation of this
nature continued throughout the Middle Ages and into the 18th
century in some areas, while on lower ground in Devon it declined
in the 15th century as pastoral farming became more profitable and
other areas suited to grain production were able to export surpluses.
On the high moors, where most people still lived in dispersed
farmsteads and hamlets surrounded by their fields but sharing the
commons beyond, marginal land was still expected to produce
cereals in rotation with grass. There is no evidence of summer farms
on Exmoor and the summering grounds recorded in Exford appear
to be large closes of improved pasture, probably watered.[56]

    In the mid-14th century an account was made of the losses
suffered by Denise de Reigny while her lands were in the possession
of John Payn and his wife Margaret. At Hawkridge she had 13
acres of fallow land, 16 acres of crops, including barley and rye,
and two meadows (37 acres) of which she lost both the hay and
the aftergrass. She also lost her Christmas, Easter and Midsummer
rents totalling £2 13s., sales of winter pasture worth 13s. 4d., cider,
perry, and the profits of her doves from the garden, and six tables,
a chest, and a trough. This would have been devastating in an area
where yields were low in the first place but it would be wrong to
conclude that the moors were an unprofitable wasteland.[57]

Grazing

The moors supported thousands of cattle and sheep besides the wild ponies and deer. We know this because of several pieces of evidence relating to animals owed in payment, or from fines for the pasturing of cows and sheep. The Royal Forester, William de Plecy, owed the king 16 heifers and a young bull each year for the bailiwick of Exmoor in the 1250s, indicating that he had a large herd there. In 1335 several manors, including Dunster, were presented at court for allowing their tenants to graze cattle in the forest without licence, and in 1362 the bailiff of North Molton manor was accused of unlawfully pasturing 60 sheep. Summer grazing for cattle was limited by the number that could be wintered on farms.

The grazing could be improved by the practice of swaling – in 1333 three men from Molton were accused of burning 1,000 acres of heath to the injury of the king's deer and in 1338 one unfortunate man was presented for accidentally setting fire to 100 acres of forest heath when swaling in neighbouring Stoke Pero. Fuel gathering also caused problems. In 1270 Henry of Ashway forfeited Ashway wood and his neighbour Hilary de Mounceaux was fined 6s. 8d. for cutting without licence. In 1333, the rector of Oare, William Cabbel, was presented at the forest court for taking oak saplings in his parish. Some upland areas relied on turbary, the right to cut turf and peat, for fuel, but this could also get people into difficulties. In 1270 seven men from Exford and Withypool were fined for making new turbaries in the forest without licence and in 1335 the lord of Oare and his tenants were

Figure 35 Evidence of earlier cultivation on Winsford hill, now covered in heath. It was possibly during the 12th and 13th centuries that large areas of Winsford Hill came under the plough and enclosures were made at Wambarrows on top of the hill. These are visible on the aerial photograph as horizontal lines of ridge and furrow and a rectilinear field system, crossed by diagonal tracks.

presented for digging turves for fuel on their own land, because it lay within the forest. In Devon, exempt from forest jurisdiction, the lords of manors allowed turbary rights to their tenants.[58]

The importance of the upland and its wild crops is reflected in several cases heard before Henry de Bracton concerning Winsford Hill. Disputes in 1251 concerned the furze crop on 100 acres, beat burning (burning the tufts of old herbage) and enclosing meadow for cattle. In 1257, 16 Winsford farmers were in dispute with the abbot of Forde over pasture, and also furze, which was valued for kindling, heating ovens, and dry hedging. Other wild crops were: berries, especially whortleberries; bracken for bedding or burning for potash; heather for bedding, fuel, and thatching; rushes and sedges for strewing floors, rush lights, and thatching; and turf for fuel and boundary banks.[59]

Figure 36 Sheep on Exmoor. The rearing of hardy livestock on the moors has changed little since medieval times. It could earn farmers a significant income. If all the free grazing rights in the forest were exercised there would have been over 7,000 sheep from Withypool and Hawkridge in addition to those whose owners paid for grazing.

The 1327 subsidy shows that upland taxpayers were as prosperous as those in the lowlands. Brushford was the wealthiest tithing, with Almsworthy a close second, and of at least 115 taxpayers in the six Somerset parishes, 48 were assessed at 1s. or more. There is little record of secondary employment, despite archaeological evidence of mining and a search for silver in the north of Brushford parish in 1312-13. Ditchers and fishermen were recorded, and there were tailors at

Figure 37 Peat cutting on Exmoor, a traditional practice at least since the Middle Ages, which involved stripping large areas of moorland.

Almsworthy in Exford, at Brushford and at Molland, which also had a soapmaker and a painter. Only neighbouring Brompton Regis shows evidence of cloth making and tanning, although the surnames Fuller and Comber, recorded in Dulverton in 1270, hint at the presence of cloth making there, and we know that a fuller and a glover could afford to lease part of the Dulverton tithes in the 1320s. The fact that Dulverton was granted a weekly Thursday market for the life of the grantees and two annual fairs in 1306 also suggests that there was commercial trade going on in the area, as does the presence of a salter in the 1330s (and another in Exford in 1348), who may have been preserving meat for sale.[60]

LATE MEDIEVAL SETTLEMENT

The Black Death and Population

The mid-14th century in Britain is regarded as a watershed between an era of good weather, growth of population and settlement, and expansion of cultivated land and a period of bad weather, poor harvests, ill health, declining population, and abandonment of marginal settlement and arable land. The situation in Exmoor did not necessarily reflect the national pattern. While the 1334 tax assessments show that Brushford, Hawkridge, and Withypool had fallen in value compared with their neighbours, the disparity may reflect the departure of resident lords. Likewise, a fall in population could possibly be accounted for by poorer climatic conditions. The dispersed and remote nature of settlement on Exmoor may even have protected it from the factor that caused the most drastic loss of population in other areas of the country: the Black Death. The outbreak of plague, which began at Melcombe Regis, near Weymouth, in 1348 and reached the north of Scotland in 1350, killed perhaps a third of the population across the country and was to be a recurring scourge from the 1360s until the 1660s. But while a few parishes had a change of priest in 1349, the only direct reference to the plague in southern Exmoor comes from a survey of North Molton in 1361, the year of the second outbreak: 'On account of the pestilence there are in the hands of the lord twenty-two furlongs of land which were in the hands of bondmen.' And even here the population loss must have been small as there were 798 poll taxpayers in 1377 and North Molton manor rents rose from £17 10s. in 1314 to £40 in 1361.[61]

The general rise in the number of taxpayers in southern Exmoor by the 1520s seems to support the theory that population losses in the 14th century were not as high as elsewhere. A comparison of subsidy returns for Brushford, Dulverton, Molland and Winsford shows interesting discrepancies. Molland appears to have lost population and taxable wealth by the 1520s whereas Dulverton's taxable population had greatly increased. Molland's tax return may be deficient, but between 1504 and 1507 eight Molland manor tenants were fined for allowing their houses to become 'ruinous and badly repaired'. William Vicary, tenant of West Lee, had neglected to maintain the chapel of St George there. Of 49 settlements listed in four of the parishes in 1327, only five had been abandoned by the 19th century, and some of those losses may have been post-medieval, or they may have survived under another name. Most farmstead desertions date from the 19th century or later.[62]

Prosperity and Community Life

The 15th and early 16th centuries saw southern Exmoor prosper, as evidenced by the surviving buildings. A relatively high number of medieval longhouses survive on Exmoor, due to their quality and isolation. Examples in Lower Sowerhill in Brushford, Badlake in West Anstey, and Edbrooke and Lyncombe in Winsford may date from the 15th century, while others in West Nightcott in Brushford, Luckesses in Exford and Cloggs in Hawkridge are later. At Molland, 16 farmhouses have been classed as of late medieval or early 16th-century origin. Their smoke-blackened timbers, solid jointed-cruck roofs (common in Somerset between the 1390s and 1630s), and good quality windows and doors show that parishioners could afford the finest work. The longhouse continued to be built in upland areas until the 17th century, probably for economy of space and masonry, although with a solid division between house and shippon (the cattle shed).

Religious buildings in the area provide further evidence for prosperity in southern Exmoor during this period. First, there are the aisles, towers and large windows added in the medieval period following the great phase of Norman church building: the 13th-century chancel and the window containing 14th-century glass at Winsford, the rebuilding of the church at West Anstey, which has altars dedicated in 1319, and the new chancel and tower that were added at Hawkridge in the 14th century. And then there is the wealth and devotion that can be read in the 15th-century church towers of Dulverton, East Anstey, Molland, and Exford, the tower and aisle at West Anstey, the naves of Hawkridge and Winsford, and the virtual rebuilding

Figure 38 Former church house in West Anstey. Some parishes, like Molland and West Anstey, built church houses, which were predecessors of the modern church hall. They consisted of a great open hall and were later divided into cottages.

Figure 39 The medieval
packhorse bridge over the
river Winn at Winsford
was restored after the
1952 flood. It carries
the road which crosses
Winsford hill to Tarr Steps.
The river Exe was crossed
by a similar bridge.

of Brushford, Dulverton, Molland, and Withypool churches. Money was spent on these buildings and, despite the absence of resident lords and the dispersed nature of settlement, parishes maintained their churches and clergy.

Finally, both trade and the sense of community would have been bolstered by improvements to the transport infrastructure in the area, an important part of which was in place by the end of the Middle Ages. Initially, an increase in trade, the movement of livestock and a desire to travel not only in the favourable summer months probably led to the replacement of fords by bridges on important routes; an essential process, since southern Exmoor provided high roads between north and south, and east and west for traders and drovers. One such route was that between Devon and Somerset, where a substantial bridge was built to cross the Barle, a river that, along with the Exe, was not easily forded when in spate. Clapper bridges like Tarr Steps can disappear under floodwater. Bridges were built at Dulverton, which stands between the Barle and the Exe and had fairs in the 15th century, while bridges at Exford and Withypool gave access to the forest and those at Winsford carried roads over the Exe and the Winn.[63]

Chapter 5

Reformation to Interregnum, 1530-1654

Figure 40
Henry VIII from a grant of Treborough, formerly held by Cleeve Abbey, 1540.

In 1530 few people in southern Exmoor could have foreseen the great changes that were to take place in the coming decade. In 1535 Henry VIII ordered a valuation of church property. The findings, known as the *Valor Ecclesiasticus*, showed the government that seizure of monastic property could provide much needed capital. That was the beginning of a relentless tide of change from which Exmoor could not escape. After 450 years of relative stability the area faced the traumatic changes of the Reformation, beginning with the destruction of the religious houses, many of which owned land on Exmoor. In 1538 the parish register was introduced, a public record of every baptism, marriage, and burial, and in 1539 the English bible was made available to parish churches. Changes in religious and administrative practices would see the parish challenge the manor for control of the local community, with tenant farmers and freeholders becoming more assertive, running local affairs through parish offices such as churchwarden. The divisions in religion and politics resulting from the upheavals of the 16th century hardened in the early 17th century, plunging the country into a bloody civil war.

THE ROYAL FOREST IN DECLINE

Life in southern Exmoor was still largely determined by those who controlled the forest, now physically confined to the area of the later Exmoor parish. Kings were no longer interested in hunting on Exmoor and were happy to leave its administration to their officials and tenants. As early as the beginning of the 16th century, the then warden of the forest, Giles, Lord Daubeney, recommended to his deputy, Sir John Trevelyan, that he permit Sir Hugh Luttrell, owner of estates bordering the forest and his (the warden's) brother-in-law, to take two deer a year. In 1508, the new warden, Sir Edmund Carew, paid £46 13s. 4d., which remained the forest rent until 1814, and was required to leave a herd of 100 deer at the expiry of his lease. Many leaseholders sublet to undertenants, like the Pollards of King's Nympton who controlled Exmoor for much of the 16th century. Robert Colshill, who leased the forest in 1568, began a conflict between local farmers and tenants of the forest, which resulted in almost continuous litigation from the 1560s to the end of the 17th century. He increased grazing charges from 1s. 8d. per 20 sheep to 2s.

Tenants of the forest refused to accept that neighbouring
parishes had been disafforested, which caused severe difficulties
for local people. The lord of Hawkridge manor impounded cattle
on Hawkridge Common but lost his case on the grounds that
Hawkridge Common was part of the forest despite the fact that
it had been disafforested in the early 14th century. Similarly, the
people of Withypool were accused of poaching fish from the queen
although they were exercising their rights as free suitors. In 1597
their lands were claimed as freeholds within the forest and they
were accused of killing deer and maintaining alehouses there.
Between 1588 and 1591 nine men from Dulverton and one from
Winsford were accused with others of poaching in groups of up to
30 with crossbows and greyhounds and of lodging deer poachers.
The possession of dogs and crossbows was justified by isolated
farmers such as John Baker 'for the preservation of himself and his
house, dwelling far from neighbours'.[64]

Sir John Poyntz, warden of the forest, alleged at a swainmote
court (see panel 4) held in Hawkridge churchyard in 1589, that
Peter Edgcumbe and 'sundry other ill-disposed persons, arrayed in
warlike manner with weapons, coats of mail and defence, pistols
charged, swords, bucklers, daggers, and other weapons as well
invasive as defensive, repaired to the said Court, and there publicly
required all the tenants of the premises that they should not
pay their rents nor do suit and service'. Poyntz also clashed with
George Luttrell, lord of the honor of Dunster and of Carhampton
hundred, claiming that the parishes north and west of the forest,
which had been disafforested nearly three centuries earlier, were
within the forest.[65]

Another source of conflict arose because the free suitors, with
their grazing rights, represented a loss of revenue to the forest
lessees. Resentment at this probably led Sir Hugh Pollard in 1608

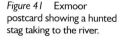

Figure 41 Exmoor
postcard showing a hunted
stag taking to the river.

to enforce the ancient duties. In return for pasture and fuel in the forest, and freedom from tolls in markets and fairs in the region, the free suitors ought, he argued, to perform nine drifts of cattle, horses and sheep that pastured in the forest each year. However, it was said that boys of 14 would be set to the work or that suitors would go on foot so animals escaped back into the forest. When this happened the forest lessees took strays for themselves from the bordering commons, unclaimed animals, or sheep not shorn at the proper time.

But the most serious of the transgressions heard at the court concerned charges for sheep grazing. The cost of grazing a score (20) of sheep was rising, reaching 2s. 6d. in 1629 and 3s. 4d. in 1637. At the same time, tithes were imposed on wool. Until then the forest had not been subject to tithes, since it was not part of a parish, which was a major motive for pasturing animals. In 1633 the Crown, anxious to raise money, claimed ownership of the tithes of the forest and let them to George Cottington, who in turn sold his lease for £2,000 to James Mills of Hampshire in 1635. Subsequently, in order to maintain his income in the face of reducing flocks, Mills secured the right to half the tithe wool, or a twentieth of all the wool from sheep pastured in the forest, and Somerset farmers had to give notice before shearing their sheep to William Tucker of Exford. Not content with this settlement, however, Mills declared that the neighbouring commons were encroachments on the forest distinguished only by stones, which might have been moved. But he does not seem to have proceeded further with this claim, perhaps because the costs of so much litigation ate into his profits.

Naturally, there was reluctance to pay the higher grazing charges, especially since sheep were already prone to being lost because of 'stealing, killing, drowning or stifling in the snow', as reported by William Thorne of North Molton. Some farmers refused to pay the full rates, and others, like William Squire, a gentleman from South Molton, withdrew their animals. This had a negative effect on levels of employment, since many servants and shepherds found themselves out of work. It also impacted on the quality of pasture because large numbers of sheep in earlier times had kept down the coarser grass. As Paul Holway of East Buckland stated, 'the lower the sedge grass is eaten in the spring, the pasture will be sweeter all year and the sheep prove the better'. Another result of the charges was that the advertisement of agistment prices became more common, as was noted in Barnstaple, South Molton, and Dunster by John Courte of Withypool.[66]

Swaling also caused difficulties. Some argued that it was a damaging practice, but in 1640 one farmer maintained that the

Figure 42 Exmoor
National Park Authority in
the process of 'swaling':
burning the old vegetation,
to improve moorland.

custom improved, rather than destroyed, the heath, and that
without it the old heath was not 'fit for deer or cattle to browse
on, being so old and overgrown that no grass grew'. The lessee
of the forest, therefore, stood to make more profit if two or
three hundred acres of old heath were burnt as was done on
neighbouring commons.

The Civil War put a temporary end to litigation and made
farmers even more reluctant to expose their sheep on the moor,
since they worried that troopers crossing the area might take fresh
mutton to supplement their provisions. Ironically, Exmoor's only
royal visit for centuries occurred in 1645 when the young prince
Charles was escorted from Dunster to Barnstaple.

In 1651 the forest was surveyed with a view to its sale and
valued at over £470 a year. It was stated that it was tithe free and
Hawkridge free suitors did not use their rights. The surveyor, a
stranger to the area, described the forest as

> a mountainous and cold ground much clouded with thick fogs
> and mists, and is used for pasturing cattle, horses, and sheep,
> and is a very sound sheep pasture, but a very great part thereof
> is overgrown with heath, and yielding but a poor kind of turf of
> little value there.[67]

However, he thought some of the hills had good soil and might be enclosed and improved, an aspiration on which his valuation was based.

In 1652 the forest was bought by Joseph Strange in trust for James Boevey, a London merchant of Dutch descent, and for the first time passed into private hands. In September 1653 Boevey wrote from South Molton to Isabella, his wife of six months, 'I am well come through the forest to our utmost station. I find all in good condition, our business goes bravely forward'. He had probably begun the building of his house at Simonsbath, which has the date 1654 on a beam. From his deeds and leases it is clear that Boevey was intending to put tenants in the forest and to oust those who 'make divers claims and pretences to receive privileges in the said Chase'.[68]

'TIS THE SHEEP HATH PAID FOR ALL?

Tax returns for southern Exmoor for the 16th century indicate that the area was growing wealthier. The 1544-7 records for Devon show a rise in the number of taxpayers compared with 1525: Molland now had 48, Twitchen, 20, and East and West Anstey, 57. England as a whole was also experiencing long-term growth in population, despite occasional outbreaks of plague and the disastrous harvests of the 1590s. Exmoor largely reflected this pattern. The plague of 1546-7 hit Barnstaple, but North Molton and other parishes on the edge of Exmoor escaped entirely and the influenza of the 1550s does not appear to have troubled many rural parishes in east Devon. At Dulverton and Brushford there were twice as many baptisms as burials in the 1560s and at Brushford there were years when there were one or no burials. This may have led to unemployment, and many vagrant families were seen on the road between Taunton and Barnstaple in the 1580s, and a few travellers were buried at Brushford, but in general Exmoor saw an increase in prosperity in the 16th century in line with the rest of the country.[69]

There remained variations in the levels of wealth between the different parishes. The 1581 subsidy reveals 10 taxpayers in Hawkridge who were assessed at £5 or less, whereas Brushford and Winsford had a few taxpayers worth between £8 and £12. Almsworthy in Exford had 23 taxpayers, Winsford, 35, and Dulverton, 48, but other than Humphrey Sydenham (a member of the family that governed the town at the time) only eight of the last were assessed at over £5. Apart from Robert Courtenay only three of Molland's 25 taxpayers were assessed at more than £5, but Twitchen had four out of 18 and the Ansteys 13 out of 27, of

Figure 43   Courtenay monument in Molland church. Like most of the Courtenays those at West Molland were Roman Catholics but that did not prevent them having a lavish set of monuments erected in the parish church. They were one of the few gentry families to live in southern Exmoor.

The Commons

Many Exmoor commons were under forest law in the 13th century. Following disafforestation manors gained control of their own commons and were anxious to maintain it. They were not always successful. In 1541 six Withypool farmers were accused at the forest court of ploughing seven acres of Withypool common with oxen and enclosing it for tillage the previous year. In 1559, after 25 men were similarly accused with regard to 10 acres, it was stated that the common could only be used by the free suitors for pasture or by stock taken from the forest at the drift or chase, the round-up of grazing stock.

We can learn about commons from manorial court rolls. Disputes were taken to the courts, which maintained common rights and punished infringements. In 1553 three men were variously accused at Almsworthy manor court of taking stone, heath, and turves without licence. In 1556 four men were ordered to make enclosures on the common before St Luke's day (18 October), presumably for sowing, and others were presented for driving animals out of the manor during the chase. Farmers depended heavily on common hill pasture in summer to make a profit from their stock, which could not hope to be as profitable as those on richer grazing. There was always a temptation to overstock to increase yields. In 1556 a man was accused of overburdening Riscombe Down in Exford with 100 sheep. Almsworthy tenants were reminded that they must abide by the

Figure A   *Corn ditch to keep sheep out of crops on the commons. Temporary fences were raised on low walls of earth and turves and removed when the commons were not in tillage. Later some were stone faced as a permanent barrier. A ditch in front prevent stock jumping over.*

Figure B *Comer's Gate Winsford. At Winsford names such as Comer's Gate, Edbrooke Hill Gate, Cross Gate, and Summer Way indicate routes by which animals were driven to common pasture.*

accustomed rate for stocking the commons. The breaking of common grazing for arable would have reduced pasture temporarily. In 1559 two farmers were fined because their grain growing in the commons was insufficiently hedged. Traces of such fields are found on Wellshead Allotment. Monkham manor common in Exford continued to be cultivated in 1638. At Winsford the church raised money by letting rights to put a number of sheep on the commons and in 1603 a cottager was allowed to graze 10 sheep if he obtained the consent of the manor tenants.

The communities of southern Exmoor had to know the boundaries of their commons. Some bounds were clearly marked such as the 'Cornell' ditch that divided common rights at Anstey in the 1530s. Others had stones or trees at intervals that needed to be memorised. Manors and parishes perambulated (walked) their boundaries. Boys would be sat on the stones, or on occasion held upside down, so that they would remember the bounds. Elderly parishioners remembered the Exford perambulations of 1606 and later because they were pinched at a boundstone. In 1623 the minister of Molland led 30 or 40 inhabitants on a perambulation of Molland Common whose boundary was marked by heaps of stones 40 yards apart.

whom Thomasina Webber and William Snow of West Anstey were assessed at £10 or more.[70]

Variations in wealth aside, many prosperous farmers rebuilt or extended their houses, adding parlours and additional bedchambers, as part of the so-called 'Great Rebuilding' during this period. The addition of bedchambers came as a result of a desire for greater privacy and comfort and was achieved by the insertion of additional floors in halls and the inclusion of stair turrets. In the case of longhouses the shippon was often converted into a parlour for private family use with the hall becoming a general reception and dining room. More rooms led to the provision of additional fireplaces and chimneys.

I thank God and evershall / 'tis the Sheep hath paid for all.

From the clothiers' prayer of thanks.

To what extent did sheep farming and the wool trade contribute to this new prosperity? Sheep were certainly a valuable commodity for the upland farmers of southern Exmoor. Henry Stote of Almsworthy was one such farmer, who could put 100 lambs on the down in 1553. And when Peter Hill of Withypool died in 1626 his farm produce comprised butter, cheese, hay, corn, geese, and livestock but his sheep accounted for over a quarter of his wealth. He also had wool, cards and spinning wheels indicating that his household produced yarn. The clergy also did well: the vicar of Winsford claimed £8 in wool tithes in 1536, approximately half his income.[71]

Most Winsford wills and inventories in the 17th century included sheep. Between 1637 and 1639 three members of the Hindham family left flocks worth, respectively, £72, £22 6s. 8d. (for 64 sheep and 21 lambs), and £54, and in 1645 John Barue left 143 sheep worth £28. The Joyce family of Dulverton appear to have bought and sold sheep among themselves and had an elaborate system of ear marks or cuts to identify their animals. Such marks were essential when sheep theft was common. There were several cases in Brushford in the early 17th century, including a glover's wife from Brushford who stole and killed a sheep.[72]

The Wool Trade

By the early 16th century wool was being made into cloth locally. In the 1520s Philip Burgys of North Molton sued Annys, executor and widow of John Hetherd of North Molton, clothier, for refusing to pay money outstanding for white woollen cloths called 'Molton whites'. These were made from Exmoor wool and may have been shipped from Barnstaple. To the south of the area Tiverton rose to prominence in the later 16th century as a cloth town exporting to London, and its merchants probably handled cloth from southern Exmoor. By 1532 Dulverton church had a chapel dedicated to St Blaise, the patron saint of woolcombers, which suggests that there were enough woolcombers by this time to warrant them having a religious fraternity of their own. Dulverton's growth in size and wealth in the 15th and early 16th centuries has parallels in villages like Pensford in east Somerset that became cloth towns in this period.[73]

Richard Skinner, a clothier from Dulverton, marketed cloths at St James's Fair in Bristol. He sold for £8 eleven dozen kerseys (medium weight woollen cloth widely made in east Devon from the late 15th century). William Westhorne bought caps and other merchandise from a London haberdasher in the 1550s but his son John preferred the bright lights of Exeter, and travelled to London on his master's business with his pockets full of money.[74]

It sounds as though the claim that Dulverton was 'in great ruin and decay' in the 1550s was an exaggeration, and it was certainly flourishing by the 1590s when market profits had risen from £19 to £23. In the same year neighbouring Bampton, held by the Earl of Bath, was said to have lost trade to Dulverton, and the people of Dulverton are thought to have been so afraid that Bampton would 'overthrow' their market that Humphrey Sydenham had to offer £100 to prevent such an event from occurring. He spent time and the town's money in London searching documents and taking advice from lawyers, and eventually won the case, despite complaints about the disposal of market revenues. The accounts were read out in church but no assent by the inhabitants to their use was allowed. Some of the revenue was for the poor, but one witness claimed that 'where before they were wont to be relieved with money and clothing of the profits of the fairs and market that now they had apples, pears and white bread'.[75]

Evidence for a thriving wool trade is also to be found in the early 17th century, with weaving in Brushford. In 1619 Martin Thomas had a weaver's shop at Exebridge, and the trade can also be traced from wills of the time. William Blackmore left a loom to his son in 1621 and in 1626 Anthony Tucker left two looms to his two sons-in-law. Also, the Sydenham family owned a fulling mill in Dulverton in 1638 and three by 1654, indicating that there was plenty of locally produced cloth to be fulled.[76]

The West Country continued to be known for kerseys until the early 17th century when serge, a hardwearing cloth made from wool and worsted, was introduced. By 1700 this had supplanted kerseys and there was no evidence of light worsted cloths being made in the area, probably because the local sheep were mainly short wool breeds. Long wool or worsted would have to have been imported. Most cloth made in southern Exmoor at this time would have passed through Tiverton to London, but by the early 18th century it was being shipped straight from Exeter and Topsham to Holland, Germany, and Spain.

PARISH LIFE, VILLAGES AND FARMS

Although most people still lived on dispersed farms, Exford, Molland, Winsford, and Dulverton developed village settlements of cottages and farmhouses near the parish church and the river crossings from this period. Those on the road to the church would also have been on the route to the mill, the alehouse, the cobbler, or the smithy, while near the river crossings are likely to have been the dwellings of craftsmen and smallholders, who would naturally make their houses in accessible places. A few good cottages of this type, built in the early 17th century, have survived. The homes of paupers and married labourers, on the other hand, might be found more often on roadside verges within walking distance of the farms where they might find work.

The proliferation of building work undoubtedly offered employment for craftsmen, woodmen, and quarrymen, but there is some evidence of a shortage of good skills and materials in remoter parts of the moor such as Exford. It is probable that this shortage was partly supplied by small farmers who supplemented their income by doing building work when their labour was not needed on the land. The large number of small quarries in the area produced the stone of which older houses were built but unusually Winsford and the western hamlets of Brushford have several cob buildings (made from clay, sand, straw, water and earth). Most houses surviving from this period are farmhouses and only one house earlier than the 18th century has so far been recorded from Hawkridge and Withypool. What survives is a fraction of what was built at the period, and the buildings we know least about are those of the poor.

Farmers probably accounted for half the population of southern Exmoor and labourers and servants for about a third. The rest consisted of gentlemen, clergy, traders, and craftsmen, many of whom would also have engaged in farming, especially resident clergy, who farmed their glebe (church land). Local magistrates fixed wages and in the later 16th century farm labourers were entitled to no more than 6d. a day in winter and 8d. in summer, half if food and drink were provided. Women earned far less and if fed by their employer would receive no more than 1d. for a full day's work. Girls under 14 worked for their food and clothing only and many unmarried farm servants would have lived in.

Divisions of farms and estates continued as the population increased. In 1556 the Almsworthy manor court allowed a tenant to build a new house on land at Imbercombe. On the same manor Pitsworthy Farm was split into Lower and Higher or Over, which was in turn divided into two. Anstey Crewes manor was divided into four and all the land was let out. In 1582 in addition to the demesne farm (273 acres) there were 14 holdings between 20 and 160 acres of which three were held together to create a 310-acre farm. Two were held with Dunsley mill and one had no house. Pairs of farms such as East and West Wadcombe and Nether and Over Radnidge, where each had the same acreage and rent, imply the halving of former large farms. Among the rents due to the manor one man paid for the right to fetch his cattle from Sterling common.[77]

Livestock were a farmer's most valuable possession and people at this time often left sheep or cattle rather than cash to children, grandchildren, friends and servants. In 1536 William Vicary, vicar of Winsford and rector of Brushford, left all his sheep and cattle in Brushford parish to the church, and Roger Nethercott of Winsford gave a kinsman a cow, two bullocks and 30 sheep. In the light of this it is easy to imagine just what a loss it must have been to his wife and children when Thomas Almsworthy of Exford gave away a dozen sheep and a cow in 1530. But it was not only livestock that were of value; elderly farmers depended on family support when they were unable to work, which is probably why in 1556 John Gregory of Exford gave his land to Robert Gregory in return for food, clothing, and fire for life.[78]

The parish church remained the focus of the community in the 1530s, with people showing devotion and piety in their bequests to

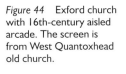

Figure 44   Exford church with 16th-century aisled arcade. The screen is from West Quantoxhead old church.

the church, as previous generations had done before them. Clergy like George Elsworthy of Exford and William Vicary of Winsford left money for prayers. Elsworthy also gave money to glaze the west window of Dunster church, his books to Cleeve abbey if a library was made within a year of his death, and all his sheep to his servant. The rest was to go towards building an aisle in Exford church to which many of his parishioners had also made bequests. The same year Richard Coppe, evidently the Exford blacksmith, gave £3 towards the aisle if the parish would begin the work within three years of his death. He left his anvil and tools to his son and a cauldron to the church for an anniversary service.

Apart from money people left livestock, jewellery, clothing, or wax to their parish church, or to fraternities (usually dedicated to a saint), which lent money in time of need or paid for the burial of members of the fraternity. One such bequest came from Frideswide Thorne of Winsford, who gave a silver ring and sheep to the church fraternities and two silver shells to her daughter. In another example, from 1557, the wool from a sheep left to Winsford church

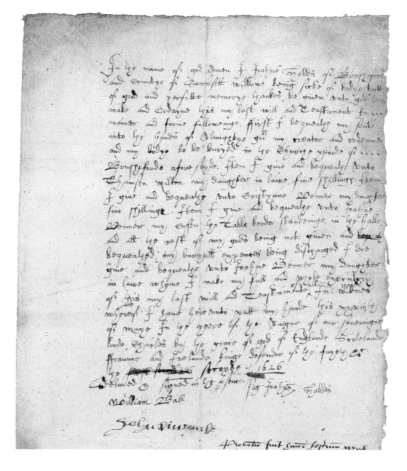

Figure 45 Will of Joan Hobbs of Brushford, widow, 1626. She left everything to her daughter and daughters-in-law except her hall table, which she gave to a female cousin.

Figure 46 Defaced image in Molland church, probably Mary Magdalen. During the Reformation many images were destroyed especially those of Christ crucified and Mary.

was sold to benefit church funds. People also made charitable bequests, which varied from almsgiving to providing benefits to the community. This was the motivation behind John Catford of Mounsey in Dulverton leaving a sheep to his local church: he hoped that income raised from the sale of it could be used to maintain the bridge.

In contrast, by the late 16th century few people left more than a token sum to charity. Roger Bradford of Dulverton is a typical example of a wealthy farmer from this period, who died in 1579 only leaving 6d. to the church and 6d. to the poor, but 10 sheep to his stepdaughter and £20 to his unborn child.[79]

Many on remote farmsteads would have found regular church attendance difficult in bad weather, so prayers, and later bible readings, at home would have assumed greater importance in Exmoor than elsewhere. The nearest religious house to southern Exmoor was tiny Barlynch priory east of Dulverton, but the changes wrought in the church by the Reformation must have shaken the conservative inhabitants of Exmoor. Local people would have been closely affected by the loss of the Mass and devotional lights and the closure of private chapels in their churches, but having no choice in the matter the overwhelming majority conformed, at least outwardly. It is not known if Exmoor people supported the Western rebellion in 1549, against the changes in the church, but at least one rebel was executed at Exford, presumably because it was on the high road across the moors. Many travellers would see the corpses, a grisly warning to discontented local people. This is perhaps why nearby Morebath was a parish that conformed obediently, despite equipping five men for the 1549 rebellion, and having a strong attachment to St Sidwell.[80]

Fear of rebellion and invasion caused parishes to maintain arms and beacons. In 1569 the muster raised 19 archers, billmen, and pikemen at Winsford but the combined parishes of Exton, Hawkridge and Withypool could only find four billmen. Almsworthy's able men included a gunner and Dulverton had a light horseman and a gunner among 24 able men. John and Thomas Sydenham each provided guns and a light horse while other inhabitants of Dulverton maintained armour and weapons. In 1596 the Winsford tithingmen had two muskets, one parishioner had a sheaf of arrows although no bow was recorded, and others had armour.[81]

Theft was the most common offence at this time, but the harbouring of vagrants was also recorded. A Winsford farmer was accused of this in 1607 (he had allowed people to stay in his alehouse). More unusual was the group of poor women who, in 1621, stirred up by a local baker, threatened to attack the clerk of

Figure 47 Molland
stocks. Petty crime was
always a problem but
at times of economic
or political crisis
maintaining law and
order could be difficult.

Dulverton market with stones. Presumably they were angry at the
price of bread and, unlike the baker, felt they had nothing to lose.

Other social problems also brought unrest. In the early
17th century Edward Byam, vicar of Dulverton, wrote to local
magistrate John Trevelyan of Nettlecombe, concerning Nicholas
Cleeve, a Dulverton shoemaker, two of whose many children were a
charge on the parish:

> … he being a shoemaker and a very good workman, not
> having wrought any thing this long time either to help them
> or to relieve himself his own maintenance is partly by stealing
> poultry and such like lewd courses, and partly by the help
> of one Humfry Chilcott who is a seller of ale and a receiver
> of such things as he lewdly gets, and in whose house he
> and such lewd company both whores, knaves & thieves are
> continually harboured.[82]

In 1556 Dulverton, claiming to be a 'town and borough' and 'very
populous', was granted a charter because 'on account of the poverty
of the inhabitants [it was] in great ruin and decay'. Under the charter
10 trustees were appointed to use the revenues received from the
market and fair to benefit the town's inhabitants. A piepowder court
(a corruption of *pied poudre*, the dusty feet of traders) was to settle
disputes during fairs and markets, and the town constables were to
provide policing, collect tolls, and redistribute the money with the
assent of the majority of the town's tradespeople.[83]

While Dulverton people may have aspired to urban status the
village was only part of a large rural parish and in practice was run
along those lines. Prosperous yeomen would have dominated the
community – men like John Anstie who in 1636 had corn worth
£40 in his barn, along with cattle, sheep, and eight plough oxen

– while most people living there were engaged in agriculture or crafts. A few went into military service, like John Crewes, who in 1608 was with Sir Thomas Roper's regiment at Limerick, but they were very much in the minority.[84]

CIVIL WAR AND INTERREGNUM

Exmoor was not too remote to escape the outcome of conflict between king and parliament in the 1640s. The outbreak of Civil War not only entailed fighting between opposing armies but also aroused latent bitterness between neighbours, and social and religious groups, possibly fuelled by rising population. A butcher's wife at South Molton is said to have attempted to throw rams' horns, which were considered to be a symbol of immorality, at a group of cavaliers.[85]

The importance to both sides of Dunster castle to the north-east ensured that Exmoor often saw troops on its roads. In September 1642 Sir Ralph Hopton's force, variously said to be anything from 160- to 400-strong, marched from Dunster to Dulverton, and then

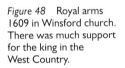

Figure 48 Royal arms 1609 in Winsford church. There was much support for the king in the West Country.

to Exford and across the moors towards Barnstaple. Subsequently troops of soldiers and supplies probably crossed Exmoor towards Dunster. There would have been an ever-present fear of looting or seizure of supplies, forced quartering of soldiers, and pressure to provide carting services. One unnamed soldier, possibly on his way to or from the garrison at Dunster, was buried at Exford in September 1643. By 1646 landowners in Exmoor who were believed to have supported the king were brought before the county committees of the new government and faced enormous fines. Although he deserted the king's cause and never bore arms, John Courtenay of Molland was fined £750, possibly because of his Catholicism. Henry Sydenham of Dulverton, despite being in arms, escaped lightly with a fine of £20.[86]

The number of ordinary Exmoor people caught up in the fighting is unknown, but after the Restoration of Charles II in 1660 many who had been maimed and impoverished fighting for his father appealed for relief. John Fisher of Molland said 'he was so hurt and wounded that he lost the use of one of his legs and thereby is now become maimed and brought into poverty'. In 1644-5 Griffin Morgan of Molland fought in one of the royalist sieges of Taunton, which played a significant role in the outcome of the war. He gave a graphic account of his experiences:

at the sieges of Lyme and Taunton and several other places, where the petitioner always manifested his true loyalty by his continual valour and diligence … at the siege of Taunton after many dangerous assaults, at last your petitioner was thrust through with a halberd in his thigh, and shot through the other thigh with a bullet all from and by the enemy, and yet was not himself taken, but took some of the enemy and brought them away; But by the said thrust and shot was so maimed, that he is disabled to get his living as formerly by his labours, having a wife and four small children.[87]

The 1640s and 1650s were a time of suffering and uncertainty on Exmoor. As with the Reformation a century earlier, community bonds had been severely strained; the parish church and the manor court, which had traditionally brought people together, both saw attendance decline, and the church ales and other entertainments were no longer being held. Several communities lost their vicars and landlords, who were deposed for supporting the king, and at Exford, which lost its Royalist rector John Hunt in 1646, a dispute broke out between two rival claimants to the living. It would not have been surprising if some parishioners had asserted themselves under such conditions and indeed, in Winsford, the churchwardens and

Figure 49 Signatures and marks of Brushford parishioners agreeing to stand surety for the father of an illegitimate child 1649 (1648 old style).

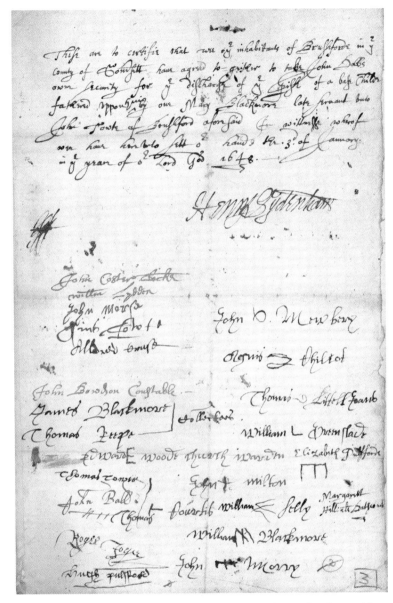

overseers, assisted by the four, later eight, men chosen by the parish, looked after the church, gave alms to travellers and maintained the poor. In 1651 they spent nearly £3 on a pauper's funeral. Most parishes appointed a registrar to keep a record of births, marriages and deaths in 1653.[88]

Chapter 6

After the Civil War, 1654-1815

Figure 50 An 18th-century shepherd taken from a map of Dulverton, 1790.

The aftermath of the Civil War left its mark on the parishes of southern Exmoor. Every community probably knew someone who had suffered injury or loss of property, and now they had to adapt to republican government and changes in the church. One such change imposed by the new government was civil marriage, officiated by magistrates such as Thomas Siderfin, who travelled around west Somerset conducting the ceremonies, including many in Brushford and Dulverton. However, there seems to have been no reluctance to return to church weddings after 1660 when the monarchy was reinstated, and it may be that some who were married in civil ceremonies at this time did not feel that their union was lawful.[89]

The agricultural year still bonded people together, but farmers began to be influenced by the interest in agricultural improvement, and the pressure to expand often squeezed out the smallholder. It would have been more difficult for the young to find land to farm when they married and the number of landless labouring families increased. After another period of war, this time against Napoleon, private estates, farms, and a new parish would replace the Royal Forest of Exmoor.

THE HOUSE IN THE FOREST

Why did James Boevey choose to build a house in the heart of Exmoor, miles from the nearest habitation? According to John Aubrey, James Boevey, an intellectual and a linguist who later studied law, retired from the mercantile business to a country life because of ill health. He wrote *Active Philosophy* and other, mostly lost, manuscripts. He was a small dark man, 'of great Temperance, and deep Thoughts, and a working head never Idle'. Aubrey added, 'In all his travels he was never robbed.' Samuel Pepys remembered him as 'a solicitor and a lawyer and a merchant altogether who hath travelled very much'.[90]

Boevey bought the freehold of Exmoor Forest from the Commonwealth Parliament in 1653 and in 1654 he raised the agistment rates for sheep in the forest to 10s. for 20, five times the rate before 1629. Farmers responded by withdrawing their animals or refusing to pay, even when the rate was reduced to 6s. 8d. in 1655. Boevey reacted by launching the first of many actions in

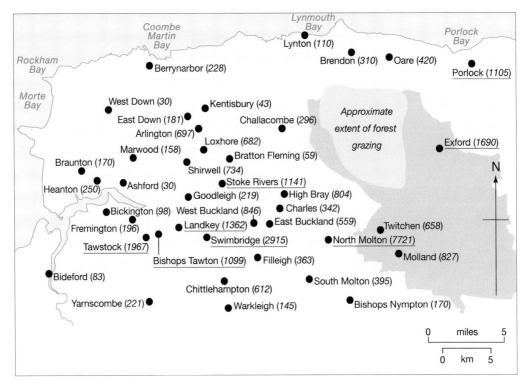

Figure 51 Map showing parish of residence of owners paying to graze their sheep in Exmoor Forest in 1736, with the number of sheep belonging to each parish in brackets. The use of forest grazing by people from North Devon is remarkable.

the Court of Exchequer concerning grazing and the extent of the forest. He targeted large numbers of farmers, whether for refusing to pay agistment rates, or for other offences, which may have included taking greyhounds and guns into the forest to kill deer.

Men resisting higher charges would probably underestimate the value of the grazing, commenting that, 'such stuff as pastures thereon gains very little thereby, other than for the preservation of their own grounds,' or that the land, 'produces a course, mossy and sour grass only serviceable to keep beasts alive, and not to grow and improve them'. But despite losses, such as that suffered by Anthony Southcombe of East Buckland in 1739, when he had sheep stolen from Simonsbath, forest grazing was too valuable to both hill and lowland farmers to be given up lightly. It was also sought after: sheep owners came from as far away as Bideford – about twenty miles from the forest – to graze their animals, and the rates for agistment in Exmoor were proclaimed at stock sales in markets, towns, and ports between Barnstaple and Dunster. The Forest Book of 1736 records that besides the 7,000 or more allowed to the free suitors there were 30,136 sheep in the forest that year; 13,941 from the neighbouring borderers or suitors at large, and 16,195 from strangers.

Boevey, for one, understood the value of the grazing, and of Simonsbath House, which Robert Pollard of South Molton

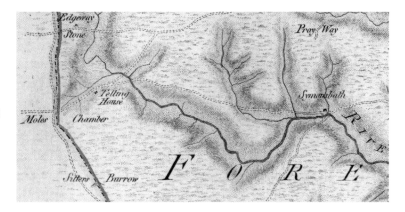

Figure 52 Map of Exmoor, 1782, showing the telling house in the west of the forest. Its ruins could be seen a century later. Men known as tellers kept a record of the sheep in the forest and checked that they had been paid for.

described as 'most convenient for all the borderers and for such as come to enter sheep and cattle and to fetch and drive them away or to pay for the agistments and tithes'. By 1657, the year of Pollard's description, Boevey had settled in Chelsea, and Simonsbath was occupied by John Hill from Withypool. Boevey's freehold was converted back to a leasehold on the Restoration of Crown lands in 1660, and residents of Exmoor petitioned (unsuccessfully) for his eviction from the forest. In 1674 after many years in Holland, some of them in prison, Boevey again turned his attention to Exmoor and continued with litigation until his death in 1696. The successor to the leasehold, Robert Siderfin, who bought it from Boevey's third wife Margaret in 1704, continued the policy. But perhaps it was inevitable that private entrepreneurs seeking to profit from the forest would clash with local farmers exercising their ancient rights.[91]

Figure 53 Simonsbath House, the original 17th-century three-room and cross passage house with porch, in the centre. A beam is dated 1654. Despite its isolation Simonsbath House was close to the medieval bridge carrying the east-west road across Exmoor over the river Barle.

Figure 54 Late 17th-
century map of Exmoor
Forest and its bounds.
As well as the landmarks
along the ancient
boundary a thick line has
been drawn around the
neighbouring commons.
The sources of the rivers
Barle, Exe, Sherdon and
Dane's brook are shown,
as is Hoar oak.

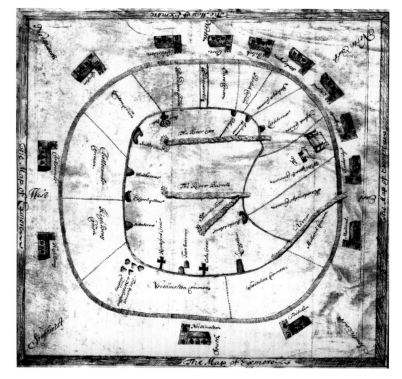

Simonsbath itself became the first farm in the forest, after
Boevey enclosed an area of approximately 118 acres, around the
house. It was farmed by the Hill family, and we know that Richard
Hill, who died in 1694, was in possession of six cattle, three pigs,
over 70 sheep, equipment for brewing, cheesemaking and salting,
and despite his residence in the forest, a gun and bows. There
was no mention of corn, hay, or wood. By 1789 it was a licensed
alehouse, known as the *Simonsbath Inn* in 1800, but it remained
the centre of forest administration and the court was held there in
the early 19th century.[92]

TRADITIONAL FARMING

The land of southern Exmoor was still a patchwork of cultivated
fields around the farms interspersed among large stretches of
rough pasture. Farming families produced eggs, bacon, cheese, beer
and cider, as shown in the lists of vats, poultry, and pigs in many
inventories. Sheep and cattle were usually the biggest outlay; few
farmers had more than 200 animals, and some smallholders had
none. John Court of Exford grew corn in 1669 but kept only an old
horse and poultry, whereas John Talbot of Brushford, who died at
Morebath in 1687, had oxen, cattle, horses, sheep and pigs worth
over £200 but no corn.[93]

Arable land was maintained. This may have been due to requirements placed on tenant farmers, such as the lessees of Combe in Dulverton in 1712, who were expected to supply 80 wheat sheaves as part of their rent. Or it may have been due to the high prices fetched by grain during the period. But whatever the cause, Highercombe Farm in Dulverton was almost entirely arable in 1750 when planned improvements included permanent hedges to replace the 'dead banks' of 'wreath and stakes'. By 1801 arable crops covered at least 17 per cent of Brushford parish, 10 per cent of Dulverton and Winsford, and six per cent of Exford, and these figures may even have been higher given that Devon farmers reportedly under stated their crops for fear of higher tithe payments.[94]

The value of Exmoor's livestock, on the other hand, certainly did not go unnoticed, as evidenced by the government's instruction that in the event of an invasion by the French, Molland drovers should take animals to Dartmoor or Somerton, avoiding roads. In fact, the economy needed moorland livestock and wool as much as lowland grain. It was Exmoor's wool that helped make Tiverton prosperous, turning it into 'the greatest manufacturing town' in Devon, after Exeter, according to Daniel Defoe. So much for the 'filthy, barren, Ground' – his description of Exmoor in the 1720s. Even when wool prices fell at the end of the 17th century the production of cattle for meat remained very profitable, so upland Exmoor was in a strong position with its mix of broad open moors suited to cattle, and steep hillsides for sheep grazing. Lowland farmers, meanwhile, valued hill country stock for breeding and fattening but often lacked the common grazing which allowed Exmoor farmers to expand production in the summer.[95]

It is evident from inventories of the period that either the farmers who practised mixed farming were more prosperous than their neighbours, or just that wealthier farmers were the ones who practised mixed farming. Some were surprisingly wealthy but lived in meagre homes. John Holcombe of Millbrook, Dulverton, who died in 1685, owned silver plate, 286 sheep, 41 cattle, 21 pigs, 12 horses, and wheat, rye, barley, peas, oats, malt and hay worth over £117. John Hinam of Dulverton, who lived in a four-roomed house but had property in Winsford, 14 oxen, six carriage horses, and 453 sheep, died in 1741 worth £3,000.[96]

Improvements introduced to southern Exmoor farms in the 18th century included gravity-fed leats to flush manure from farmyards into gutters cut along the slopes of fields, and 'bank barns', developed in Cumbria in the 17th century. Surviving bank barns can be seen at Marshclose, Hawkridge and West Nethercott, Winsford. The 'Devon Linhay', a feature of south-west England,

Figure 55 Marshclose bank barn, Hawkridge. Two-storey bank barns were built into slopes enabling easy access to both levels. The top level was used to store hay, corn, straw and fodder and the ground floor sheltered animals, whose food and hay straw could be easily thrown down through a trapdoor.

also developed in the 17th century. Its open front allowed hay to dry above pens to shelter livestock.[97]

But in general the area still lagged behind in terms of agricultural improvements. Hawkridge was said to be mostly waste covered with erica, fern, and wild thyme in 1783, while at Withypool, hill land was still cultivated for wheat, oats, and turnips, and peat was cut for fuel. There were no carts or wagons, as the roads were barely passable for horses, and oxen were still used in husbandry. Even in July the weather could be too inclement for pony sales to be held at Simonsbath with its unimproved roads.[98]

In 1794 John Billingsley reported to the Board of Agriculture on the possibility of turning Exmoor Forest, 'a useless and void space in the map', into 'as fair a prospect as the surrounding country'. He pointed out that nearby parishes had surplus labour and that with improved roads a small town or village could be created at Simonsbath with several farms.[99]

Alternatively, Charles Vancouver, Devon surveyor to the Board of Agriculture in the 1800s, thought the moors should be burnt and drained, or at least that men with capital and estates should set an example as to how the land could be improved. He noted

Probate Inventories

Until the reforms of 1837 the proving of wills was the responsibility of the church courts. Before a will could be proved an inventory had to be made of the deceased's personal property including cash, certain leaseholds, and outstanding debts. One of the purposes of the inventory was to determine the probate fees, so the inventory was valued. It did not cover everything but included saleable items. In urban areas great detail is given of household furnishings and of business stock and tools. The appraisers who drew up the inventory and valued the goods were often fellow traders or craftsmen; in rural areas they might be farmers unable to identify items who used phrases such as 'the stock in the shop' or 'his working tools'.

Many west Somerset inventories survive for the 17th and early 18th centuries and provide us with a striking glimpse of the wealth of Exmoor's farmers and craftsmen. Farming inventories contain details of household possessions and livestock. A few inventories of craftsmen and traders throw light on their tools and business. Whilst less rich in worldly goods than lowland households, Exmoor yeoman farmers at the time were prosperous and some, like John Hinam of Dulverton, were wealthy. Some invested money in property or lent it out at interest like John Pearse of Winsford whose only valuable possession was a clock. In spite of improvements to famers' homes, surviving inventories reveal little about furnishings. Even prosperous farmers appear to have had few items of furniture, perhaps an indication of thrift.

In rural areas less attention was paid to the house and its contents except for items of pewter, silver, or

Figure B   *Late 17th-century spoon by Thomas Dare of Taunton.*

brass. Country people's wealth was usually in their livestock and crops, or for a widow or retired farmer, life savings let out at interest. Over a third of the value of Alice Hole of Winsford's modest inventory was a debt of £2 10s. She possessed only bedding and a few items of furniture. Peter Burge of Hawkridge may have been a retired farmer as virtually all his worldly wealth of £22 was laid out in two houses and a bond.

Some residents of Exmoor clearly had very little to interest the neighbours who compiled the inventory. More comforts are included in Dulverton inventories, but this may owe more to the priorities of the appraisers who valued such things. By the late 17th and early 18th centuries many homes contained carpets, cushions, looking glasses and warming pans.

Figure C   *Inventory of Andrew Sedgburrow, Dulverton blacksmith. He was owed as much money as his household goods were worth. Apart from his bellows and anvil there were reap hooks that he had made. Someone in his house spun wool and he had three pigs.*

Figure A   *A Somerset brass cauldron, dated 1710, an everyday item in Exmoor farmhouses to heat water over the fire. For many farmers this was a period of prosperity and their kitchens were well stocked with brass and pewter.*

that some farmers were more interested in the livestock at fairs than in improving their land, while others had to let their grass because they could not afford livestock. He sympathised with those who worked like labourers and lived little better, whose houses were dirty, who were frugal and sparing, and who had not improved their capital. He recognised that they were producing crops as they had done for half a century and were reluctant to risk change.[100]

Successful farmers, on the other hand, aspired to be gentlemen in the late 18th century: the Lyddons of Edbrooke, Winsford, sent two boys to boarding school in Taunton. William Lyddon painted and wrote poetry and songs while Robert Lyddon's diary for 1811 records his work alongside his labourers, shooting, social visits, attendance at fairs and markets, travel to Barnstaple and Bridgwater, parish meetings, and the distribution of Christmas alms to the poor. A partial inventory of Edbrooke in 1800 shows how far they had come. There was a parlour furnished with blue and white china including tea and coffee cups and dessert plates, ivory handled cutlery, a pier glass and a Pembroke table.[101]

DULVERTON: GROWTH AND INDUSTRY

Dulverton's growth was fairly slow between the 16th and 19th centuries. Although it described itself as a 'town and borough' in 1556, there was no borough and the town was governed by the Sydenhams, whose manor courts were held in the 'Court House', probably the upper floor of the corn market house, on the site of the present Town Hall. In 1633 Thomas Gerard described it as a little market town, and by 1732 the market had generated enough money for the town to buy a fire engine. The market, which was only one of several around Exmoor, had a shambles – a row of butchers' stalls – until the 19th century.[102]

In the 1780s Dulverton had 191 houses and about a thousand inhabitants, of whom only eight were freeholders. Most dwellings were in the two main streets but about forty were scattered about the parish, of which 33 were farms. The rate of progress may have been slow, but there was perhaps more evidence of improvement here than in other parts of southern Exmoor: the paved town streets had channels of water, several shops, five public houses, and in the High Street there were quality detached and terraced houses. Older houses were divided into cottages.[103]

Population and poll tax data for the 17th century provide an added snapshot of growth in Dulverton at this time, and about what life might have been like for the people living there. In 1641 there were 226 males in Dulverton over 18, but only 98 taxpayers in

1642, and a similar pattern is seen in the 1660s, when 357 Dulverton adults paid poll tax out of a total population of possibly 600. These discrepancies might be explained by the fact that the town had many landless tradesmen and labourers. The returns from the 1660s also show that about forty families included adult children, who perhaps had not had the opportunity to leave and maintain their own farms. In addition, most of the 39 people taxed on wages were servants, although many female servants paid poll tax only, presumably because they did not earn enough to be taxed on their wages. Up to 45 households had servants, but most were probably farm workers. The town also had a small community in the 17th century of individuals who were providing services for the hinterland around. Among the bridegrooms entering civil marriages there between 1653 and 1660 there were seven weavers, four carpenters, four shoemakers, three tailors, two glovers, two butchers, a barber, a miller, a mercer, a soapboiler, and an ironmonger.[104]

The layout of the town, with its irregular, winding lanes giving it the appearance of an overgrown village, also made it difficult to imagine growth taking root. It was already cramped by the time new housing was built in the 18th century and the existing tenements themselves were bursting at the seams. Workshops often took up one of only two downstairs rooms and space had to be saved by the use of furniture that could be cleared away after meals or used as work surfaces. In bedchambers low truckle beds could be pushed under the principal bedsteads during the day.

Figure 56 The 18th-century grave of Edward Shupcott, woolcomber of Molland. In 1693 William Hensley of Hawkridge, worsted comber, leased a cottage at Molland moor, probably Lyshwell, with a garden and hopyard.

It is impossible to determine the size of the cloth industry in the Dulverton area but there is evidence to suggest that it went into decline relatively rapidly after becoming established. In 1654 there were three fulling mills, and although they were not as valuable as the four corn mills, they are evidence of a cloth trade. But by 1796 a visitor reported seeing 'several' Dulverton fulling mills in ruins. In the 17th and 18th centuries at least 15 Dulverton men styled themselves as merchant, mercer or clothier, and eight as woolcombers. A few weavers were also recorded. But by 1841 there was only one woolcomber in the area and his family were silk workers. In the mid-18th century Dulverton is known to have supplied coarse woollen cloth and blanketing to markets at Tiverton and Crediton, but by the 1780s trade with these towns had declined. Many people at Exford were still employed in cloth-related trades and crafts in 1801, but only a few were left by 1811. The main reason was that the woollen mills of the west and north of England could produce cloth more cheaply.[105]

As well as a cloth industry, there is also evidence of paper milling and of a leather trade. There was a tanhouse in Dulverton in 1654, and tanners, fellmongers, glovers, and shoemakers were recorded including John Turrell, tanner, who died in 1683, leaving a few tools, a mill with bark, and wet and dry leather worth £15. And while some of the individuals involved in industry did better than others – Robert Gibson, a coal merchant, was described as a gentleman when he died

Figure 57 Extract from the inventory of John Budd, a wealthy carpenter, who died in 1721 worth £477. He had investments but was still actively engaged in carpentry. Wood was stacked in his courtyard, meadow, garden, and barn and he had prepared timber for ploughs, gates, and building work.

Figure 58 Bilbower, originally Bilboa, High Street, Dulverton. Now a doctor's premises, as it was for most of the 19th century.

in 1791 – for most it was a struggle. Many craftsmen were also part-time farmers like William Thomas, a barber surgeon who died in 1682, with livestock worth more than his stock in trade. Probably also typical was John Dobb, a tailor with a family to support who was accused in 1698 of stealing a pair of shoes and a loaf of bread from a local farmer.[106]

In contrast with the harsh realities faced by these people, the learned Humphrey Sydenham had the luxury of an interest in global affairs. This seems to have informed his penchant for naming streets and houses as Queens, Kings or Princes, streets in London such as The Strand, Throgmorton, and White Hall, or places like Tangiers, Dantzig or Rotterdam. At 'New Battleton', a planned early 18th-century settlement on the west bank of the Barle south of Dulverton bridge, houses were called South Sea, Caspian Sea, East India, Lisbon, Morocco, Japan and Mount Atlas. A house opposite the present Town Hall was described as Guild Hall on a deed of 1776 but not in a deed of 1649, and there is no evidence that Dulverton had a guild, so this may be another of Sydenham's re-namings. The name survives and the building houses a heritage centre.[107]

LIVING AND WORKING ON EXMOOR

Figure 59 A 1689 map of Withypool and Hawkridge showing four houses and pound near Hawkridge church.

The population of southern Exmoor grew well into the 19th century, with only Hawkridge appearing to have experienced a decline; this brought a new set of problems for families. As population increased some large family farms were divided in an attempt to provide for several sons, and smallholdings were created to provide subsistence for family members. Evidence for

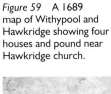

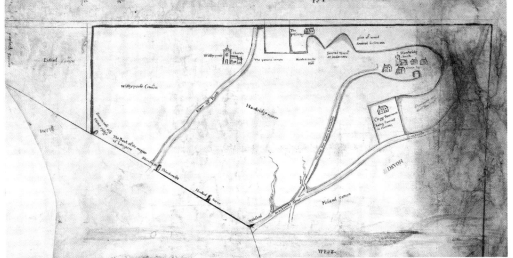

Figure 60 Population
1641-1801.

Parish	1641—2 Protestation returns: males over 18.	1665—6 Poll Tax	1744 Devon Visitation	1780s Rack's survey for Somerset	1801 Census (house-holds)
Dulverton	678	357		1,000	1049 (212)
East Anstey	102		115		165 (33)
West Anstey	168		170		215 (40)
Brushford	264	99		330	303 (62)
Exford	303			315	375 (68)
Hawkridge	90	65		75	72 (14)
Molland	324		405		473 (101)
Twitchen	144		150		145 (25)
Winsford	400	216		170	503 (91)
Withypool	153	138		170	144 (35)

Table 2: Estimated population 1641-1801

The above table shows population estimates based on five different measures. The estimates in column one are based on the assumption that the Protestation Returns represented about a third of the total population. The estimates in column two are based on the assumption that Poll Tax returns, which only exist for Williton Hundred and may have been incomplete, represent two thirds of the population. The figures in the third and fourth columns are based on vicars' estimates of families assumed to average five members including servants.

this can be seen in Molland, which had 42 farms and 14 cottages in 1545, but 63 farms and 20 cottages by 1733. People were also forced to build nearer to the church, or onto green or waste ground, as was the case in Molland, possibly Hawkridge and in Brushford, where by the 1780s ten of Brushford's 66 houses lay close to the church. Despite the splitting of large farms and the creation of new smallholdings, it was still more difficult for adult children to leave home, marry, and farm their own land. This could be the explanation behind the fact that Hawkridge had 25 single adults in 1664, excluding servants, compared with 34 in couples. There was also little alternative employment, especially for the unskilled. Many younger sons eked out a living as labourers but others must have left the area, such as the son of a local clergyman, who in 1690 was in the East Indies, or the wealthy farmer's widow and her two sons who by 1707 had emigrated from Dulverton to America.[108]

Exmoor had been quarried and mined for centuries, mainly for iron but also limestone, copper, lead, and silver. Speculator Michael Wynston was allowed to dig for minerals in 1550 and the 'Roman Lode' working west of Simonsbath has been ascribed to him, but

Figure 61 Late 17th-century Hele Bridge farmhouse, Dulverton, a three-storey, double-pile or square house built for a prosperous family. This house type allows for two reception rooms and a private parlour, and also attic bedrooms for servants. It is a vernacular interpretation of high-class housing of the period.

may be earlier. In the 1780s there were said to be ancient iron pits and slag heaps one-and-a-half miles east of Exford church.[109]

In 1675-6 a company of London men, with George Peppin of Dulverton as their local agent, dug a lead mine at Brushford, having a licence to search for gold and silver. They broke up the land, cut down 14 acres of wood for smelting, and diverted a spring of water from a farm. Not surprisingly the landowner, John Ayshford, sued for £100 for trees and 1,000 casks of lead ore. Men from Dulverton and Morebath were employed digging, washing and carrying the ore to be smelted and one miner earned 7s. 6d. a week; a high wage for the period. However, the venture was not a success. Thomas Dare, the Taunton silversmith, assayed ore from the area but found less than half a gram of silver in 16 pennyweight of lead, and the company reportedly lost £600 on the enterprise in total. It had not been a lucrative enough process: washed lead ore was worth only £37 a tun and it took 1,000lb of ore to produce 100lb of metal.[110]

The improvements in houses and farmyards, and the building of new cottages would have created a demand for stone. By the 18th century most farmhouses would have added a parlour and many were extended to provide kitchens, dairies, and servants' rooms. Some craftsmen and tradesmen could also afford a higher standard of living, reflected in the new cottages built in this period at Battleton, Dulverton, and Winsford. In 1707 a carpenter from West Anstey leased a house and land at North Lyshwell, Molland, on which to build a house.[111]

Exmoor is not suited to the grand houses and grounds to be found in lowland Britain but there are some that were built in

Figure 62 The 1805 house at Pixton Park, Dulverton had ten bedrooms and nine attics, a park, stables, lodges, stretches of water, hot and succession houses, and farms enclosed to 'appear as Pleasure Ground'. It reputedly cost £40,000 and was equipped to provide enormous hospitality on hunting days.

the area. The Musgrave's house at Stone in Exford, described as a 'pretty mansion' in the 1780s, shows fashionable architectural features, while West Molland house was extended and improved for the Courtenay family, Combe in Dulverton for the Sydenhams, and Pixton for the Aclands; in 1796 Pixton was modern and on a site of 'high picturesque beauty'. It also became fashionable to have a 'hunting box' on Exmoor, and the late 18th-century Aclands, who are said to have cared for little but hunting, had kennels at Highercombe and Jury in Dulverton. Pixton, Stone, and Highercombe had grounds that blended into the wild landscape and their owners had their main estates elsewhere.

Early Travellers

Wealthy farmers like the Lyddons of Edbrooke or the occupants of Ashway and Hele Bridge in Dulverton dominated the everyday social and political life of Exmoor, while communities were largely self-contained farming units. However, the opening up of Exmoor to tourism, if only for the wealthy, by end of the 18th century connected remote communities with the wider world. Likewise, improved communications brought new fashions and ideas to the area through letters, books and newspapers.

Getting around was still a problem. There were good medieval bridges, some of which had been rebuilt, but roads were unsuitable for wheeled traffic. Lanes and fords, which were barely passable in the winter and spring, were busy in summer and autumn with sheep and cattle moving to and from the commons and local markets. Farm inventories of the time seldom refer to carts but to packsaddles, since packhorses had to carry produce out of Exmoor and imported goods and lime to the farms. Keeping goods and produce clean during transit must have been difficult.

The first crucial change came when the Minehead road was turnpiked in 1765 and the section though Dulverton to Oldways End was turnpiked in 1786. There was no attempt to build turnpike roads across Exmoor but there were turnpike gates at the junction of Jury Hill and High Street, and at Battleton. Those improvements benefited Dulverton, but only from the 1820s, when the Minehead road was moved west into the Exe valley, making Winsford and the farms along the Exe more accessible to wheeled traffic. As well as making travel between different parts of southern Exmoor easier, increased wheeled traffic through Dulverton, especially following the widening of its bridge in 1819, provided work for blacksmiths, wheelwrights, gatekeepers and road menders. Carriers moved people and goods to and from distant towns and markets, and tourists found their way to Exmoor.

Figure 63 Rebuilt in the 18th century, the bridge at Exebridge links Somerset and Devon.

Visitors to the area, or travellers passing through, could find accommodation at alehouses. Dulverton had 10 licensed premises in 1790 including the *Red Lion*, the *White Lion*, the *Ram*, and the *Lamb*. The *Royal Oak* at Winsford probably became an inn in the 18th century when the building was extended. Inns also sometimes served as auction houses: in 1795 the *White Hart* at Dulverton was the venue for the sale of four farms and about 540 acres of land in Exton.[112]

Religion

Even before the turnpikes southern Exmoor was not beyond the reach of outside influences including religious and political dissent. After the Restoration of king and bishops in 1660, Exmoor clergy of a Presbyterian persuasion left their parishes to become travelling preachers. In 1669 six Dulverton houses were licensed for worship. Up to 300 people attended, but only two contributed to the costs. By 1710 dissent was flourishing. A 'large and commodious' Presbyterian meetinghouse had been built on the site of a weaver's cottage and the 200 or so members included 'persons of the first rank'. A major supporter was carpet maker Thomas Moore (*d.*1788) who was born in Dulverton and left money to support the chapel, Sunday school and minister. There was also a group of Quakers meeting in a malthouse in Dulverton in 1757.[113]

Figure 64 The 18th-century interior of Molland church. It was restored during the Victorian era but the altar and rails, pulpit with sounding board, box pews, and most unusually, a chancel screen survived to give an insight into a flourishing church of the period.

Methodists, however, faced opposition. A landowner near North Molton threatened to turn them out of their work and farms. As late as 1810 at Winsford 'the people, being notoriously wicked, the preachers were in continual danger of being stoned'.[114]

The 18th century is sometimes seen as a low point in Anglican church life with pluralism and non-residence leaving remote rural parishes receptive to nonconformist preaching. Devon visitations and descriptions of Somerset churches make dismal reading. At Hawkridge the church was 'very damp and nasty being much fitter for a stable than a place of worship'. However, Molland church was refitted in the mid-18th century.[115]

Charity and Sunday schools were established in a few parishes to improve basic education. Small private schools catered for the children of farmers and tradesmen, such as the young gentlemen's preparatory school at Hele Bridge or the 16th-century school at Knowstone, which presumably Molland boys attended. These schools were beyond the means of the poor who in any case needed their children's labour. In 1742 the Rev. John Norris founded a charity to educate 20 poor Brushford children. Exford's charity school taught 10 children in the 1780s but had closed by 1818 when 12 children attended a day school at Winsford and a further 12 a Sunday school there. For most Exmoor parishes there was no educational provision for the poor until the mid-19th century.[116]

Poverty

The quality of life undoubtedly improved for some farmers and craftsmen but most people survived by living off the land with few inputs from outside. The fortunate had a decent cottage and garden, regular employment, a basic education, and took an active part in parish life. Others, able to find only casual work or disabled by infirmity or old age, were condemned to a life of poverty.

In the late 18th century conditions deteriorated and poor rates rose dramatically. In many parishes of north-east Devon the poor accounted for 40 per cent of the population, and the numbers of people looking for work kept wages low. The official wage for a Devon labourer was 12d. a day, 5d. or 6d. if food was provided. An extra 4d. was paid during harvest because of the long hours. Women were lucky to earn more than 6d. a day, although they could earn more if they lived in, as could all servants. Wages were barely 50 per cent higher than in the late 16th century, yet the cost of living had trebled. Inflation rose sharply in the 1790s with the outbreak of war and even the farm servants with live-in positions, which provided them with sufficient food, clothing and warmth, found it difficult to support themselves.

It was clear that traditional subsistence farming could not provide for a growing population, or the large, possibly increasing,

Figure 65 Dulverton Sunday school card 1791. At that period Dulverton had a Sunday school and a charity school for 18 boys and 18 girls. In 1818 around seventy children attended Dulverton's charity school.

11ᵗʰ MAY, 1761.

Broke out of his Majefty's Goal,

At *Wilton*, near *Taunton*, in the County of *Somerfet* ; in the Night, between the *Nineteenth* and *Twentieth* Days of *April* laft, with two other Prifoners fince Re-taken,

GEORGE PEARSE;

Committed for Returning from Tranfportation before the Time limited.

THE faid GEORGE PEARSE is about fixty Years Old, and five Feet five Inches High ; has a large Face ; a flat Mouth, which, when he Speaks, is drawn rather to one fide of his Face. He has loft all his fore Teeth, and ftammers in his Speech ; leans very forward in Walking ; his Legs bending outwards ; has Black Hair, which hangs loofe about his Ears : Speaks Lifping, and had on (when he went away) an old Blue Coat, Leather Breeches, and White Stockings.———He pretends to be a Farrier, and to underftand and Cure Diforders in *Bullocks* and *Sheep* ; and generally carries with him fome Papers, fhowing what Cures he pretends to have Wrought on Cattle.

HE was born at *Withypoole*, in the County aforefaid.

Whoever Re-takes and Secures the faid GEORGE PEARSE, (fo as he may be brought back again to the faid Goal) fhall receive *Three Guineas* Reward, with all Reafonable Expences, of GEORGE STRONG, Keeper of the faid Goal ; and all Magiftrates and Peace-Officers, are earneftly defired to Search for the faid Delinquent, in their feveral Precincts.

NORTON, near *TAUNTON*: Printed by J. PILE.

Figure 66 Wanted notice for George Pearse of Withypool. Poverty and low wages may have drawn some people to crime.

number of landless labourers who had little opportunity for regular employment or education. Many, such as Henry Bass of Dunster, who had worked in Winsford and Withypool as a daily labourer, were forced to apply for poor relief, and overcrowding was rife. In 1801 Twitchen, Winsford, and Exford recorded around 1.3 households for each house, while West Anstey, Exford, Twitchen, and Withypool had over five persons per household, when the average was between four and five. Twitchen was the highest at 5.8, including live-in servants or labourers.[117]

Perhaps the last words on Exmoor for this period should be those of Edmund Rack who surveyed Somerset in the 1780s. He deplored the want of agricultural improvement but admired the 'wild waste intersected by deep winding Valleys, and romantic hollows'. He especially admired the 'beautiful surface' of the hills around Exford in summer and autumn. He noted 'the Erica and Hawkweed tribes; the Digitalis, blue Scabious and yellow Tormentilla, intermixed with some scarce Lichens and Polypodys; which with their blended tints enliven the scene and delight the Traveller'.[118]

Particulars

OF

A FREEHOLD FARM,

BELONGING TO HIS MAJESTY,

AND OF

The ALLOTMENTS (Tithe Free) made to His Majesty,

ON THE

INCLOSURE of EXMOOR FOREST,

IN THE

COUNTIES OF SOMERSET AND DEVON

To be Sold by Public Tender,

ON

The 23d Day of JULY, 1818,

VIZ.

	A.	R.	P.
THE FARM, called SIMON's BATH FARM, situated within the said Forest, (which Farm is inclosed, and separated from the uninclosed Lands,) containing by Estimation..............	108	2	0
THOSE several ALLOTMENTS of WASTE LAND, situated in the Center of the said Forest, contiguous and adjoining to each other and to the Farm above mentioned, and numbered on the Map 32, 33, 34, 35, 36, 37, 38, 39, 40, and 41, and containing in the whole...	10,262	1	6

IN ONE LOT.

Twelve Acres of Land to be reserved for the purpose of erecting a Church thereon agreeable to Sect. 76 — of the Enclosure Act — The Situation thereof to be agreed upon between two persons — one to be nominated by the Crown & the other by the Purchaser & in case of difference by an Umpire to be settled by the persons first chosen. The property is sold & subject to payment of one of

Chapter 7

The Exmoor Experiment, 1815-45

The new century saw England emerge from the struggle with Napoleon, and southern Exmoor no doubt joined in the celebrations for the victories at Trafalgar (1805) and Waterloo (1815). Indeed, Brushford paid out 10s. 6d. on thanksgivings celebrated with ringers and singers, probably accompanied by the church band. Lower prices for food and textiles followed the privations of the war years and the government was becoming more interested in the everyday life of the nation. There were enquiries into education, charities, and agriculture, the abolition of tithes in kind, and parliamentary enclosures, and it was the latter which affected Exmoor most closely.

After centuries of royal control, however distant, the common land in the forest of Exmoor was taken into private ownership (enclosed) and sold under an Act of Parliament passed in 1815. The forest courts ceased and those claiming rights as free suitors and suitors at large were provided with allotments from the Forest in exchange for customary pasture, fuel and fishing rights. Large landowners such as the earl of Carnarvon, Sir Charles Bampfylde, and Thomas Thornton acquired most of the allotments, which were only awarded to landowners and lessees for life. But they were insufficient compensation for many small farmers who depended upon the multiple resources the forest had provided, and for those who had held their farms on leases for years there was no compensation at all.

THE ENCLOSURE OF EXMOOR FOREST

The award and map drawn up under the Act for enclosing Exmoor Forest show that all those with rights were allotted small pieces of land around the edge. In the north-east larger sections were awarded to the owners of Porlock manor and to Sir Thomas Acland in lieu of the tithes of the forest. The rest, about half (10,262 acres), including Simonsbath Farm (108.5 acres) comprised 'his Majesty's allotment', which was offered for sale in 1818. Most North Molton farmers received a small portion of land, but many Devon estates did not (presumably because they had failed to exercise their grazing rights for some time) and Oare received nothing. On 12 May 1819 Exmoor was disafforested and on 15 March 1820 John Knight completed his purchase from the

Crown for £50,122. Some 1,000 years of royal possession had come to an end.[119]

John Knight and Simonsbath

John Knight, landowner and industrialist, sold Lea Castle, Worcestershire, to finance his Exmoor purchases. Having obtained half the total extent of the original Forest, he immediately bought up much of the rest of the allotted land. Most landowners would have had no use for a small piece of moorland remote from their other lands, too small for profitable grazing and expensive to enclose. The costs of the enclosure award must have been considerable and the additional burden of fencing would have crippled small farmers. Soon Knight owned over 16,000 acres, four fifths of the original Forest, and the manor of Brendon to the north-west. His first task was to enclose his property and turn the ancient tracks across the moor into 22 miles of road at his own expense. And then, with the help of Irish labourers, he built a 30-mile wall around his new estate. He dreamt of creating a new expanse of productive farmland but in the interim continued to accept sheep for grazing for 1s. a head. Other than sheep, only Sir Thomas Acland's ponies were allowed on his land.

In 1818, as a condition of his purchase, John Knight was required to set aside 12 acres for a church, parsonage, and burial ground. He did nothing towards fulfilling this condition, possibly because he wanted to be free of tithes and rates. The site was used for pony sales instead.

Simonsbath, still the only house on Knight's estate, stood near the junction of the road from Exford and west Somerset with those from Lynton, Combe Martin, and Barnstaple, the latter crossing the Barle at Simonsbath bridge. John Leland mentioned the bridge in 1540, the earliest use of the name Simonsbath. It was evidently an ancient and important crossing place. The road north of the river originally passed through the curtilage of the house but in the 19th century was diverted down to the river and later taken in a curve between house and river leaving the house in an elevated position.[120]

Knight probably moved to Simonsbath House in the late 1820s although he spent little time there. He was preoccupied with plans to build a mansion house, a project he spoke about to the *Taunton Courier*. Work on the house may have begun by 1822, when Greenwood's map shows foundations for a garden or tree nursery, but it was never completed. A tall north-east wing was built onto the existing house which survived until the early 20th

Figure 68 Simonsbath Farm in 1818 when Knight purchased it. It was presumably a small grazing farm and part of the property had been used as an inn. Many people had lived there in the late 18th century and possibly the house had been divided.

century. A tower on the Lynton road, now a ruin, was part of a folly or landmark on the approach from Lynton where Knight lived for several years.

Knight's dream of a mansion surrounded by a productive farm led him to search out livestock which had become more profitable than corn since the end of the Napoleonic wars, and lime to improve the soil. He also created a large park in the Barle valley stocked with fallow deer, later destroyed when they became a nuisance, and plantations to shelter the house. He had hoped to inherit a large estate whose income would have supported further work at Simonsbath but was disappointed. In 1837 he moved to Jersey, on account of his wife's ill health, leaving Simonsbath in the hands of his son, Frederic, to whom he eventually gave complete control in 1841.[121]

Other houses were built in the old forest. John Sanger of Whitechapel built one in 1818 that later became known as Ferny Ball Farm, and by 1821, when the population was 113, there were seven others. The first farms were Cornham and Honeymead, both south of the main route from Exford to Combe Martin, two miles west and east of Simonsbath respectively. Inns were also opened, of which the Sportsman at Sandyway survives. They would have been patronised by Knight's labourers and their remote position on the Somerset side of the county boundary no doubt facilitated smuggling and breaches of the licensing laws.

Altogether some 2,500 acres of land was broken up and sown in the 1820s and 1830s. Pinkery Pond, a large expanse of water on the far western edge of the former forest filled by damming the river Barle, was made and a leat dug to convey the water eastwards. The purpose for this is unclear, but it was possibly intended to irrigate the moors.[122]

The best improved land was intended to produce crops and the rest to be grazed by large herds of cattle and sheep. The investment in paring the turf, burning, liming, then deep ploughing with oxen to produce crops was enormous but the climate at 800 feet (240 metres) was not suited to corn. Cattle had never been kept in the forest all year round and the 700 highland cattle, which Knight bought in Scotland in 1826, ran short of food in winter. However, the herd was maintained for about twenty years and at first sold at a premium in local markets. But in 1841 the animals were 'wild and some were wicked' and impossible to drive to market, going off in all directions, tossing and goring everybody they met. Eventually they were shot in the fields. The 200 Herefords that Knight bought were not a success either and Devon reds and shorthorns were introduced by the 1840s. Overall, cattle proved profitable and sales in 1840 totalled £7,000. The local Exmoor sheep, although hardy, produced coarse wool which Knight could not sell for a decent price so he experimented with Cheviots and Merino using a rotation of grass and roots. His lack of success was in part due to the lack of good local shepherds and to theft. The deer were also poached in large numbers.[123]

By 1841 more labour was employed on the holding. Most of the 116 men and 47 women recorded were single workers who lived together in cottages or boarded with the married labourers. Eleven labourers boarded in one cottage and the average cottage occupancy was six. Another 100 men slept in the Exmoor district from Monday to Friday. They would have looked after the livestock on the moor and tended the arable crops. Apart from the steward at Simonsbath, only one farmer was recorded, William Carter, who later created a successful family farm at Crooked Post. A mason was the only craftsman. *Gallon House* and *Moles Chamber* were public houses on the east and west boundaries of the district. The total number of dwellings was 28, of which one was unoccupied.[124]

Frederic Knight changed the policy of the estate from direct farming with labourers to large tenanted farms. He hoped to

Figure 69 This traditional open, pillared linhay with adjoining stable at Simonsbath, may be the earliest farm building in the former forest. Since this picture was taken in 1984 the linhay has been converted into a café and the roof slated.

Figure 70   Warren
Farm, built 1844-5, one
of several new farms
built by Knight and let
around 1844 including
Emmet's Grange,
Horsen, Wintershead,
and Crooked Post.
Warren Farm covered
500 acres and employed
six labourers in 1851.

attract men with capital and experience committed to modern
methods and improvement, so he advertised widely, but especially
in the east Midlands. At first all went well. In 1842 Honeymead
with 2,100 acres was taken at £740 and in 1843 a new farm,
Simonsbath Barton, north-west of the house, was let with
cottages and 1,030 acres for £439 a year, both on 12-year leases.
At Honeymead, Somerset and Dorset dairymen managed 180
dairy cows and Southdown sheep but the flock, later replaced
with Exmoor horn, ate the cow pasture because there were no
fences between the improved and unimproved grass. Eventually
Honeymead was used as a summer farm because of the high cost
of overwintering livestock.[125]

William Hannam from North Cheriton near Wincanton in east
Somerset, who was persuaded to move to Exmoor in 1844, wrote
an account of his experiences there. It was a good summer and
'Crops in the upper Country were all Burnt up – But on Exmoor
the Crops of Corn & Grass were abundant and as fine a Harvest
as ever was known'. In September Hannam attended a sale where
everyone spoke highly of the prospects for farming on Exmoor.
He saw 'the Beautiful Crops of Corn they were just beginning
to harvest and everything looking so prosperous.' He decided to
lease land at Cornham where a farm would be built with a barn
and a waggonshed to accommodate the large quantities of corn
and hay it was planned to produce. Mr Knight usually agreed to
let land to a tenant and then built a farm for him.

Unfortunately the winter was bad and the spring so cold
that the farms were not ready for their tenants at Ladyday (25
March). 'Things now had quite a different appearance from the
September previous – there had been a Deal of Cattle lost During

the winter and a great Deal that was living looking miserably Bad
… the Forest was looking very Barren not a Green Blade to be
seen '. Many new farmers were discouraged and tried to give up
their leases but Hannam, although obviously anxious, decided to
persevere. He and his family stayed at Simonsbath House until
a cottage was prepared for them, their farm being unfinished.
Other families had the same experience. Four farmers left, but
Hannam, like many new arrivals, was convinced he could farm
there. 'There is on Exmoor every thing that Nature need provide
to bring it into Cultivation'.[126]

BREEDS OF EXMOOR

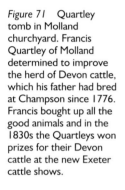

Figure 71   Quartley
tomb in Molland
churchyard. Francis
Quartley of Molland
determined to improve
the herd of Devon cattle,
which his father had bred
at Champson since 1776.
Francis bought up all the
good animals and in the
1830s the Quartleys won
prizes for their Devon
cattle at the new Exeter
cattle shows.

Selective breeding was crucial to a farmer's business on Exmoor.
The practice produced the present Exmoor Horn, a hardy animal
well suited to life on the moors and the mainstay of Exmoor
farming at this period. Its ancestor may have been the Porlock
Horn, probably a cross between the old Exmoor and Welsh sheep
shipped into Porlock in the 17th century. In 1839 small Porlock
sheep were kept at Dulverton on the exposed commons but the
better flocks were taken off in winter.

Selective breeding was also essential for producing higher
quality wool. Exmoors were cross-bred with imported Downs,

Figure 72 Exmoor Horn ewe and lambs, a hardy breed well suited to life on the moors.

Leicesters, and Merino to produce finer wool at Molland and Dulverton, and George Peppin of Dulverton took his sheep breeding skills to Australia where he developed the Peppin Merino. The particular breed of sheep not only affected the quality of wool produced, but the quantity: at East Anstey in 1842 horned sheep produced 5-7lb. of wool each, but the 'knot' or hornless breeds produced 6½ or 7lb.

One of the most striking examples of selective breeding in England occurred at Great Champson Farm in Molland, where the Quartley family revolutionised cattle-breeding. They improved the native breed of cattle, the Devon, raising its profile, but they also changed the business model that operated in cattle farming in the area at the time. Several farmers in Molland and Twitchen bred quality herds of Devons and instead of obtaining the majority of their income from selling stock at two to four years old to lowland graziers, they would maintain their herds of dairy cows. This became the norm around Dulverton. The pioneer of breeding Devon cattle, James Quartley, even had two young men of independent means living with him in 1841, who were no doubt learning about his methods.[127]

Figure 73   Red Devon
Cattle. Such was the
enthusiasm for the
improved breed that there
were nearly half a million
Devon cattle by the late
19th century, more than
any other breed apart
from the shorthorn and
there was a Devon Cattle
Breeders' Society.

FARMING IN THE PARISHES

Although much money and effort was put into livestock, farmers
were still expecting, with the aid of lime, to produce heavy corn
crops. Riphay in Brushford was provided with a new barn,
linhay, and byre; a new mill was built at Garliscombe, Withypool,
which still had 1,000 acres of arable land; and several houses and
farmsteads were enlarged including Ashway in Dulverton which
also had a new barn. In 1840 arable was still very extensive in
Twitchen and Molland, which had 1,700-2,000 acres each. Most
parishes had plenty of good grassland although common grazing
still predominated in the high moor parishes. At East Anstey nine-
and-a-half acres of furze was returned for tithe, an indication that
it was still valued. Other land use was also important: Dulverton
had over 1,000 acres of wood, water meadows were recorded at
Withypool, and orchards at Molland and East Anstey.[128]

Between 1838 and 1842 the area was extensively surveyed in
preparation for the replacement of tithes by cash payments. Most
surveyors spoke of the lack of capital investment in improvement,
the need for lime, the poor arable crops, and the absence of tithe
barns. In most areas the arable lay above the treeline between
the wooded valleys and the open moor and only a fifth of arable
in some parishes was cropped annually, chiefly for oats, wheat,
turnips, barley, and potatoes. Grain was grown for the straw to
feed stock, as meadow hay was usually sold. Only at Exford did
the surveyor refer to the common sheep walk as valuable and

appreciate the healthy pasture used for breeding young cattle for sale. He noted that the road to Dunster had been much improved by the rector.

The survey also uncovered certain ancient labour services. At Molland each farmer owed the vicar a day's work with a man and a two-horse cart, while the vicar waived tithe pigs from parishioners who would rear a hound for him. At Twitchen, a poor parish where the vicar had died, 'the utmost has been exacted for tithes' but the farmers were harassed for payment.

The surveyors noted that Withypool was inaccessible and that property values there were depressed because of the difficulty in removing produce to market. Much was spent on lime but the crops were light and ripened six weeks later than elsewhere. It was the same at Hawkridge, where the commons were grazed only in summer and the stock was disposed of or sent to the lowlands in winter. At West Anstey the roads were narrow and steep and liming was expensive because it had to be brought in. At Brushford well over half the parish was arable (1,752 acres) growing wheat, barley, and turnips, yet the crops were poor and the low prices threatened to throw much arable out of cultivation. In all, the nine parishes returned survey totals of 10,550 acres of arable, 15,368 acres of grass, and 14,592 acres of common. The acres of arable returned for Somerset is probably an underestimate because it did not include land left fallow. Livestock estimates from seven parishes totalled 21,900 sheep, 800 cows and heifers, 2,785 young cattle and bullocks, and 1,123 horses and colts, presumably mainly Exmoor ponies.[129]

In 1844 Lees tenement in Twitchen was largely arable although the land was poor, stony, cold and steep and worth as little as 10s. an acre compared with 30s. to 50s. for meadow and 30s. for orchard on the farm. Wheat continued to be grown at Winsford in the mid-19th century despite the altitude

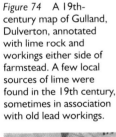

Figure 74 A 19th-century map of Gulland, Dulverton, annotated with lime rock and workings either side of farmstead. A few local sources of lime were found in the 19th century, sometimes in association with old lead workings.

Deserted Farmsteads

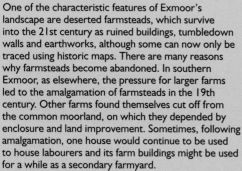

Figure A   *In 1910 Higher Prescott cottage was in fair condition with a slate roof. It comprised a kitchen, pantry, larder and two bedrooms, with a dilapidated wood house, a colt shed with loft above, and a pigsty. Later in the 20th century it was abandoned.*

Figure B   *Surveying the remains of Higher Prescott. It was a barton and 33 acres in 1839 but a small house must have been built shortly afterwards. In 1851 it was a dairy and by 1871 it was a labourer's cottage with only three habitable rooms.*

One of the characteristic features of Exmoor's landscape are deserted farmsteads, which survive into the 21st century as ruined buildings, tumbledown walls and earthworks, although some can now only be traced using historic maps. There are many reasons why farmsteads become abandoned. In southern Exmoor, as elsewhere, the pressure for larger farms led to the amalgamation of farmsteads in the 19th century. Other farms found themselves cut off from the common moorland, on which they depended by enclosure and land improvement. Sometimes, following amalgamation, one house would continue to be used to house labourers and its farm buildings might be used for a while as a secondary farmyard.

Most desertions took place in the later 19th and 20th centuries, but some were earlier. Innercombe in Exford had a decayed house by 1827. Yellowcombe farm in Winsford, recorded in 1786, was cottages shared between two neighbouring farms in 1839 and four cottages in 1871. A pair of cottages was later converted into a single dwelling, but the rest of the site is derelict.

A small unnamed farm on Holmoor at Exford was abandoned c.1840 as were Castle Farm in Hawkridge and Road Farm at Winsford. Other small farms became agricultural labourers' cottages about the same date,

including Slade in Hawkridge. Riscombe in Winsford was two farms in 1839, but shortly afterwards became two labourers' cottages. The same fate befell Mousehanger in Winsford, occupied by the 13th century. By 1786 it was without a house, but a farmstead was built before 1839. By 1841 it had been divided into two cottages. The labourers probably worked at neighbouring Lower Leigh farm, which may have utilised the farm buildings. Mousehanger became a smallholding in the 20th century and was finally abandoned when the occupants died in the 1950s, surviving in a ruinous state as recently as 1985.

Amalgamation of neighbouring farms also began in the 1840s. At Staddon in Winsford there were three farms with different owners in 1839, Little, Middle and Higher. The first may have been known as West Staddon in 1689 when it had a new barn, formerly a bakehouse. By the mid-19th century they were amalgamated as Higher, later Great Staddon (about two hundred acres), but the buildings at Little Staddon remained in use for the rest of the century. Such amalgamations gathered pace in the late 19th century, making several farmsteads redundant. The practice of having labourers living in the farm probably reduced the need for cottages, so many farmhouses were demolished for their materials or allowed to fall into ruin.

and thin soil, which was often washed from the roots and
was contaminated with a weed grass that often overwhelmed
the crop. Oats were usually grown first, followed by wheat to
improve yields, then turnips, wheat again, and finally grass
which was left till full of moss and coarse grass. The ground
was broken up with mattocks after a preliminary ploughing
and the poor arable could only be maintained by liming. Lime
was produced around Molland and West Anstey in the late 18th
century but not in sufficient quantity to supply demand. Lime
for Exmoor parishes was shipped in through Barnstaple or
brought up from Watchet, Bampton or Tiverton.[130]

COTTAGERS AND LABOURERS

Southern Exmoor's population rose by 37.5 per cent between
1811 and 1841. What is most surprising is that the biggest growth
was at Exford (50 per cent) and Withypool (72 per cent). The
smallest growth was at Twitchen (10 per cent). Even allowing for
inaccuracies in the early census, some parishes were experiencing
unsustainable population growth. The average household size
across the area in 1841 ranged from 4.65 in Hawkridge to six
or more in Molland, East Anstey, and Winsford in 1841. Two
Molland farmhouses had 15 or more residents and in Winsford
large numbers of labourers were squeezed into farmhouses or
lodgings: a shoemaker had three apprentices living in his cottage.
Labourers with several children made room for lodgers, usually
other labourers, but one had three sweeps and an Irish traveller
boarding. There was also a shortage of houses in several parishes
in 1811 and 1821, by which time, if the census figures are correct,
over a third of houses in Exford were shared. And the steady rise
in population was not halted by disease, although Dulverton
was struck by cholera in 1834. Of 46 deaths, 32 were of children
under 10, mainly the under fives who were most vulnerable to
dehydration and diarrhoea. Neighbouring Brushford was not
affected until the autumn, where nine of the 13 burials that year
were children under ten.[131]

Exmoor was in the lowest wage area of England in the early
19th century so it is not surprising that labourers could make
no provision for sickness or unemployment. In 1815 in the
10 parishes of southern Exmoor, 258 people received regular
poor relief and 87 received poor relief occasionally. The figures
do not include those who received private charity money. No-
one was in a workhouse and there were no friendly societies.
Proportionally more people were on casual relief in Devon,
and Twitchen had no-one on regular parish pay. Based on

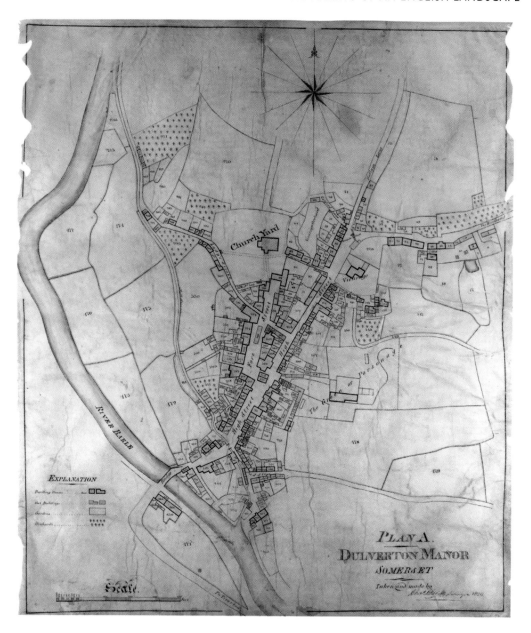

Figure 75 Dulverton town in 1820, hardly changed since 1790. Despite an increase in population there seems to have been little house building. Between 1810 and 1816 there were many homeless paupers who were housed in inns, including the *Ram* and the *White Horse*, at parish expense.

1811 population figures Dulverton had the highest proportion of people on regular relief with nearly 10 per cent, followed by Molland, West Anstey, Exford, and Winsford with around eight per cent. Hawkridge had the lowest figure at two per cent, but that reflects the difference between settlements with large numbers of cottages and the dispersed parishes comprising mainly farms.[132]

Winsford was a parish of poor cottagers. In 1821 only 66 of the 97 families were employed in agriculture, and between 1815 and 1835 Winsford overseers spent around £230 a year, mostly in relieving the poor. They maintained a parish poorhouse and paid rents of paupers in their own homes. In 1830, 20 households were on regular relief and in 1833, 34 households were on permanent or temporary relief. In 1841 a quarter of Winsford's population consisted of male agricultural labourers, compared with 14 per cent at Hawkridge where the poor house had only one inmate.[133]

John Clatworthy, confined to bed in 1835, is an example of one man's rise and fall. He was born in Winsford, but aged nine went to work for Mr Lyddon of Edbrooke for six months, and after that with Robert Lyddon of Morebath for 11 months, returning to his parents with a dislocated arm. After working, presumably as a groom or ostler, at the *Feathers* inn in Minehead and then for a clergyman, he again returned to his parents. His wages rising with every move, he worked for a Wiveliscombe attorney, a man at Crowcombe, several places in Bristol as under ostler, and for Mr Everard of Stone, Exford, for 20 guineas a year. After six months with Rev. Philip Wilson of Exford for only 12 guineas a year, he returned to his father who employed him for 2s. a week, board and lodging.[134]

Under the new poor law of 1834 workhouses were to be built for parishes grouped into poor-law unions. The Devon parishes were placed in the South Molton union, and the Somerset parishes in the

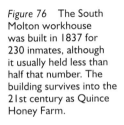

Figure 76 The South Molton workhouse was built in 1837 for 230 inmates, although it usually held less than half that number. The building survives into the 21st century as Quince Honey Farm.

Dulverton union. The Dulverton workhouse was not built until 1855, so until that date Dulverton union provided weekly outdoor relief.

Many recipients were not living in the parish that was responsible for relieving them. In 1840, of the 39 Brushford claimants, nine lived in Devon; of 178 people relieved at Dulverton, 19 lived in Taunton, Bristol or elsewhere, and at Hawkridge only one of five claimants lived in the parish. In Winsford 111 people, of whom 18 lived elsewhere, received relief – this was nearly a fifth of the population of the parish. Across the six Somerset parishes 79 men usually received 1s. a week, 134 women received 2s., and 8½d. a week in bread, and 204 children under 16 received 6d., and 8½d. a week in bread. Of the children, 24 claimed independently of their parents. Most applicants were turned down but policy was not consistent. Fathers out of work because of the weather in 1841 were turned down for relief in Brushford but given money in Winsford. Applications for extra money or bread were usually refused but those requesting blankets or clothing, medical and funeral costs usually got something. Most applicants were widows, unmarried mothers, labourers, and Dulverton shoemakers. Among the more unusual applicants were a sick Dulverton man whose wife lived in Wales and a mason from Hawkridge who had returned to his wife from prison. Bills presented to the union included a doctor's bill in excess of £10 for a Dulverton lunatic in Taunton Asylum and a demand for reimbursement from Plymouth union, which was maintaining an Exford widow.[135]

There was little employment for the growing population, particularly women. They could find some casual work on the land but there were few dairies, traditionally a source of female employment. However, a few worked as dressmakers or straw plaiters and there were opportunities at the silk factory that had been established at Dulverton by 1828.

From the second decade of the 19th century the silk industry spread to rural Somerset, wherever there was abundant water and young female labour. Girls, aged between 11 and 15, earned 2s. to 3s. 6d. a week in the 1830s in the industry and some were their family's main breadwinner. The census of 1841 recorded 44 silk workers, including 29 weavers, in Dulverton. Apart from a girl aged 10 who worked with her mother and a lady of 60, they were all girls and young women aged from about 12 to 30 years old. A few were lodging, some were single mothers, but most were local and there were many groups of sisters in the trade. By 1851 the 42 silk workers included married mothers, who had presumably grown up in the trade. Young girls from 10 were employed as winders.[136]

Dulverton had still not become a focus for southern Exmoor. Its market was small, the market house was much smaller than

Figure 77   Last meeting of Dulverton Friendly Society, founded in 1816, September 1968. Poor relief compared unfavourably with friendly society payments. A Winsford member got 6s. a week. His widow, on relief, had only 3s. 6d. for his doctor and 3s. a week with bread for herself and three children.

the present Town Hall, and although there was a large shambles building in the middle of Fore Street, in 1839 it was said that most produce from the area was sold in Tiverton and South Molton. A hatter, milliner, grocer, druggist and two shopkeepers were recorded in 1841 but most traders and craftsmen were such as would be found in any village.

Nonconformity

Village life was expanding in the 19th century as the nonconformist chapel and the village school were added. Nonconformity reached maturity and respectability in the 19th century and

Figure 78 Dulverton laundry, reputedly built on the site of the 18th-century blanket factory. It was a silk factory from the 1820s until the 1860s and appears to have produced crêpe and lace and used handlooms. It was water powered by 1861.

many communities supported both church and chapel. Although the major nonconformist influence on Exmoor is regarded as Methodism, with its later offshoot in the Bible Christian movement, it was not until the mid-19th century that it was successfully established in Somerset's Exmoor. It was never strong in Dulverton but there were groups of Methodists there, and at Winsford, Withypool, and later in Exford. Methodism has a longer history in the Devon parishes of Twitchen and Molland. The Lyddon family of Twitchen, who were millers and blacksmiths – the craftsmen to whom Methodism appealed – were early converts and two generations were preachers; the elder William Lyddon in fact died in 1852 on his way to preach at Oldways End, where the chapel was built in 1845. The family set up a meeting room in the cottage at Twitchen mill in 1828 and later a chapel was built over the stables. There was a small pipe-organ, a rarity in the area, which was shown to visitors to raise money for the Methodist missions. The younger William Lyddon was a staunch Wesleyan Methodist until his death in 1898 at South Molton where he had a music business.[137]

By the 1840s southern Exmoor was experiencing both increasing population, from 3,444 in 1811 to 4,572 in 1841, and the amalgamation of farms. Some farmers looked to the new techniques and machinery, combined with better access to meat markets, to increase their income, but many were pushed out of farming and could not find work. It is no surprise that in the decades to come the trickle of leavers would be become a regular outflow. And it was not just the uprooted farmers who were seeking their fortune elsewhere, it was the young and ambitious, especially those with a basic education from Sunday school and access to newspapers, who were looking to the world beyond Exmoor for work and betterment. Those who stayed no doubt looked for other opportunities to improve their lot such as mining, the railway, and ultimately tourism.

Chapter 8

The Rise and Fall of High Farming, 1845-1910

Figure 79 St Luke's Church, Simonsbath. The first incumbent, W.H. Thornton, was instrumental in bringing to justice William Burgess who murdered his daughter.

Southern Exmoor was transformed in the later 19th century, as agriculture and industry benefited from developments in the wider world. The railway brought in new materials and fertilisers and took livestock and meat to distant markets, while machinery, powered by horses or water, was introduced on the larger farms. There was further amalgamation of farms, and some were deserted, but for redundant labourers or small farmers who had lost their land possible openings became available in the revived mining industry. Communities benefited from improvements to common moorland and the building or rebuilding of many churches, chapels, schools, houses and farmsteads, but for many it was the era of emigration from Exmoor.

THE MAKING OF EXMOOR PARISH

Frederic Knight, unlike his father, was more interested in creating tenant farms than in directly farming a large estate. As a result, it is no surprise that there was an increase in the number of farmsteads on his land from 10 in 1848 to 22 by 1851. These included Tom's Hill, a 300-acre model farm with house and farm buildings around a courtyard, and Larkbarrow. Many such buildings went up, but they did not always endure: indeed, Tom's Hill and Larkbarrow were easily reduced to rubble during the Second World War.

The 20-year leases Knight offered were divided into periods of four years, and in the early periods rents were lowered to allow for investment in lime (used as fertiliser) and reclamation, provided annual accounts were submitted. As in the east Midlands, where many tenants came from, Knight also allowed compensation at the end of the lease for investments.

Many of the tenant farmers met with success. Robert Smith from Lincolnshire, who was the Knights' land agent for 20,000 acres, made his home at Emmett's Grange, where he farmed 674 acres and employed 15 labourers and four boys in 1851. He drained a bog by deep ploughing, grew rape and roots to feed cattle, pigs and horses, and pared and burned land before ploughing and liming for arable cultivation. Improvements cost him over £4 an acre and he acknowledged that the land was more suited to grass but he recommended his methods. He planned

Figure 80   Emmett's Grange, Exmoor. The best of Frederick Knight's (below) farms, it comprised a large house with service wing, a barn, stables, and outbuildings round a foldyard. There was rough summer pasture on the hill tops, arable land on the slopes, and meadow pasture in the valley bottoms.

a six-course rotation of roots and two corn crops either side of three years of grass.[138]

Other farmers were less successful. Mr Meadows from Leicestershire succeeded in producing Stilton cheese but failed to grow wheat at Larkbarrow and had to sell up in 1852. William Hannam of Cornham, who took up his lease in the 1840s, faced a similar problem. He had a herd of Devon cows and produced butter and Cheddar cheese, but he had difficulty selling his produce in the 1850s. He ended up penniless, humiliated, and apparently lost his mind. Tenancies remained erratic. Some tenants never set foot on their premises, while one farmer could not cope and committed suicide.[139]

Exmoor farms were generally far larger than those in neighbouring parishes, and some also included dairies, such as the farm at Winstitchen. Of 17 for which acreages are known in 1851, seven were over 300 acres, and Larkbarrow and Horsen were over 800 acres. Larger farms required greater numbers of staff, including bailiffs, shepherds, herdsmen, and grooms, but 18 men and 15 women had recently left because there was no work for them.

The population in 1851 was 275 and still rising. Most workers lived with their families but there were two houses of single labourers, as well as 15 empty houses including Honeymead Farm. These people needed a place to worship, and Exmoor residents petitioned the government for a church in 1845 and 1853, citing the distance to Exford, which was five miles along a poor road. Eventually, in 1856, St Luke's Church opened. In 1857 Exmoor became a separate ecclesiastical parish, and in 1858 it became a civil parish. Once the church had been built other services came to the area, and by 1891 Simonsbath had a school, blacksmith, carpenter, masons, dressmakers, a hotel, which doubled as a farm, and by 1901 a post office.[140]

Upland Challenges

Hard winters on Exmoor in the 1860s killed many hill ewes and poor summers reduced the turnip crop, and therefore the market weight of sheep. But gradually a system of agriculture suited to the hostile Exmoor weather evolved. One breakthrough came in 1877 when the steam-powered Sutherland plough, used to reclaim moorland in Scotland after the highland Clearances, cleared 400 acres of Exmoor, some of it underwater. As part of the process two large ploughshares cut furrows in the peat a foot deep and two feet wide, and a subsoiler on huge wooden rollers broke up the pan below the peat, enabling water to drain away. Other new agricultural practices included the combination of cross ploughing and harrowing with lime, which enabled two or three rape crops to be grown for fattening lambs. The soil was then able to support permanent grass, although liberal applications of lime were needed.[141]

The increased demand for meat from urban areas, combined with the arrival of the railway in 1873, made Exmoor stock rearing profitable. Hill lambs provided particularly good business, as they were said to be of superior flavour. They were bought at Simonsbath or driven to South Molton between August and November for slaughter. They were then taken to London for sale in special meat vans. Attempts to extend the season by growing kale for the sheep were not successful.

By the 1870s three quarters of farm tenants were former labourers familiar with the moorland. Others were Scottish shepherds, who had stayed on after establishing sheep herdings there. In 1880 Frederic Knight wrote:

Figure 81 The road bridge over the River Barle at Simonsbath. Although believed to be medieval in origin, this three-arch bridge has been rebuilt several times subsequently, most recently and extensively after the flood of 1952.

I know of no part of England in which so large a number of agricultural labourers have risen from the actual plough tail to the position of farmers and masters in the same County in which they worked as men, as in the north of Devon and the adjoining district of Somersetshire. I take from my own rent roll the names of Blackmore, Carter, Comer (2), Elworthy, Fry (2), Hayes,

Steer, Crowcombe, Locke, Pile (2), Ball, Richards etc … paying me … together the annual sum of £1,270 … all of them within my recollection agricultural labourers, excepting two whose fathers rose from the ranks equally within my remembrance; and these rents are without any arrears and paid regularly to the last shilling. Several of these men who began life with little or no education, and with nothing but their heads and their hands to help them, occupy land to a considerable amount in adjoining parishes and under other landlords.[142]

Land Value

The late 19th-century agricultural depression affected Exmoor less severely than the lowlands. Evidence for this can be found in a report on Frederic Knight's estate, published in 1882 by William Little:

I have given a rather full notice of this estate, not only because it is interesting as a record of agricultural progress, and progress still continued and maintained notwithstanding all discouragements, but also because it is a real relief to myself to write, and it may be the same to some to read, of a district where agricultural depression is a thing unknown.

He compared Exmoor with Pawlet Hams near Bridgwater, one of the richest grazing lands in the South West and formerly let for high rents. But at Pawlett there were no improvements, farmers had gone bankrupt and rents had been remitted.[143]

Conversely, on Exmoor, cattle breeding remained profitable, despite the fact that the availability of cheap imported livestock led

Figure 82 Sale of Exmoor ponies at Bampton Fair, 1860.

to a fall in meat prices. Exmoor sheep were also successful. They escaped foot-rot, which was extensive on the lowlands in the cold, wet year of 1879, and the costs of keeping the sheep were low, so farmers were able to stay in business even when wool prices fell and New Zealand lamb pushed prices down. Depressed corn prices enabled farmers to buy feed and smallholders survived because they relied on family labour with little outside help.

In 1886 Exmoor supported 290 dairy cows, 594 other cattle, 225 horses and ponies, 14,144 sheep and lambs, 54 pigs and over 1,200 poultry. Oats, rape and other fodder crops were grown but potato growing declined to three acres by 1906 when there were over 6,600 acres of permanent grass of which 570 acres were mown. Of the 1,219 acres of cultivated land, 653 acres was under clover or artificial grass. The number of farmers increased from 28 in 1876 to 42 in 1906 as farm sizes reduced. Heavy horses outnumbered ponies, there were more than twice as many dairy cows and pigs than in 1866 and sheep flocks had increased by a third with 7,443 breeding ewes.[144]

The 1910 valuation of southern Exmoor's farms reveals a certain amount of good practice and some prosperous businesses. Farms near Simonsbath were 'useful', Cornham was well managed, and in East Anstey old cob and thatch farmhouses like medieval Bungsland were in good condition with land of fair quality. In Molland and Twitchen courtyard farmsteads were common, many barns had horse engines attached and Kerswell had an open-air horse gin. The tenant of Blindwell in Twitchen was singled out for keeping the buildings in good repair, and a stable was being built at the courtyard farm at Higher House, whose farmer kept about 240 cattle on around 800 acres. He and his neighbours used a lot of lime and artificial manure.[145]

However, for the most part, the men making the valuations were not impressed; the lack of investment was noticeable. Picked Stones was a 'very rough farm', 'rather inaccessible' and in a 'very exposed situation with no sheltered fields in winter', while Yaney's modern farmhouse was badly built. A 2,383-acre allotment was used to breed Exmoor ponies, but two others over 1,000 acres were unhealthy sheep runs. The best that was said of any holding was that it was 'productive in summer' or 'fairly productive for the district'. Buildings were generally in a better state, with stone in a 'fair' condition and slate often tarred to keep the rain out. But certain houses under 60 years old were so bad they were thought to be very old and one farm was an uninhabited ruin. Cottages, often single storey, were dilapidated, damp, and even ruinous, and Simonsbath Post Office was barely habitable. In some cases, large farmhouses were let separately while the farmer was provided with a cottage.[146]

Exmoor Farmyards

The severe winters and wet summers, which are characteristic of English upland regions like Exmoor, limited the potential for arable cultivation and created an economy based on rearing livestock. The farming year on Exmoor therefore required seasonal movement of animals to make maximum use of grass growth during the summer months and to provide the livestock and cultivated crops with shelter from Exmoor's climate during the winter months. These harsh conditions and changing seasonal requirements created a distinctive type of farmyard on Exmoor during the second half of the 19th century.

The farmyards were clearly influenced by the model farms of the mid-19th century whose buildings were arranged in a logical sequence to maximise output. The larger storage buildings were often positioned to provide the uncovered yards with added protection from the elements. The upland topography was utilised in the form of bank barns which were terraced into the hillside so that the upper floors could be entered from ground level and the lower floor from the yard. The steep slopes provided a sufficient head of water for waterpower to be harnessed to drive the threshing machines and chaff cutters vital for turning the summer crops into manageable lengths for cattle and horse feed.

The hill farming year required the farm buildings to be adapted during the different seasons. The reconstruction drawings opposite show Ashway Farm, Dulverton, as it may have looked at the end of the 19th century. In the summer the sheep would have been driven to the farm for sorting and shearing, making use of the cart store and upper yard and possibly buildings which would otherwise be in use for the cattle. Several Exmoor farmers testify to the use of threshing barns for shearing sheep (Lyshwell, Stetfold Rocks and Silcombe). In the winter the cattle were housed and fed in buildings around the main yard, including the shippons below the threshing barn in the west range and the granary in the north range. This was when the threshing machine and chaff cutter, powered by a waterwheel and launder, were used the most, preparing food for distribution to cattle and the horses stabled in the east range. During the winter, sheep were kept on pastures close to the farm and although Exmoor horn sheep could lamb outdoors, less hardy breeds needed lambing sheds. The only known purpose-built lambing shed at Exmoor is at Stetfold Rocks.

Farms like Ashway were also heavily reliant on horses, which had replaced oxen and ponies as the principal draught beasts on Exmoor in the 19th century. Shire horses were expensive to house and feed and could not be left outside like the native ponies so purpose built stables, such as those which form Ashway's east range, also became a common and prominent feature of the Exmoor farmyard.

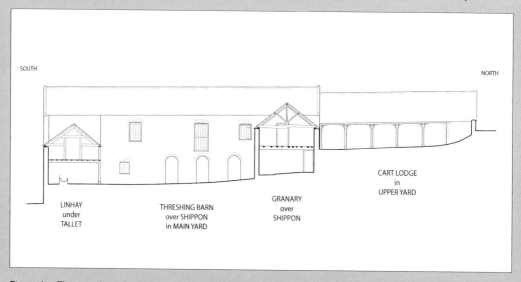

SOUTH

NORTH

CART LODGE
in
UPPER YARD

LINHAY
under
TALLET

THRESHING BARN
over SHIPPON
in MAIN YARD

GRANARY
over
SHIPPON

Figure A   The east elevation of the west range at Ashway farm, Dulverton. The principal range of buildings at Ashway was terraced into the hillside to allow carts to enter the threshing floor at ground-floor level whilst still allowing cattle access to the shippon from the yard. The waterwheel pit and metal launder were situated behind the threshing barn and were replaced as the farm's motive power by a tractor in the 1960s.

Figures B and C   Reconstruction drawings of the yard at Ashway during the summer and winter seasons. The new yard was arranged to give protection to livestock and crops from Exmoor winters and enable fodder to be distributed efficiently under cover.

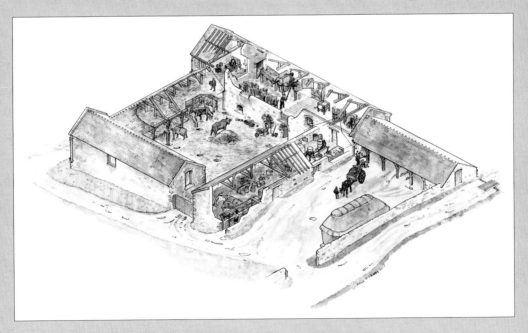

SOUTHERN EXMOOR FARMS

After Exmoor Forest was enclosed there was inevitably pressure on neighbouring commons, and those at Dulverton, Exford, Hawkridge and Winsford were enclosed between 1848 and 1859 at great expense. Enclosing a 10-acre field could cost £40. Moorland was vital to the farm economy and few new farms were created outside Exmoor parish.[147]

Agricultural improvements favoured large farms and many small- to medium-sized holdings were amalgamated with their neighbours. Farms which went out of use between the mid-19th and mid-20th centuries, probably as part of such amalgamations, included Streamcombe, Lower Marsh, and Lower Spire in Dulverton; North Newland, Higher Pitsworthy, Sharcott, and Lower and Higher Prescott in Exford; Kingsland Pits in Exmoor; and Higher Leigh and Pine Farm in Winsford. But many landlords found small farmers were better tenants and several large farms created by mid-19th-century amalgamation were divided in the 1890s.[148]

Farmhouses on enlarged farms were also rebuilt or improved. Riphay farmhouse in Brushford and Liscombe in Dulverton were rebuilt in the 1850s and Landcombe at Lyshwell in Molland, let to William Buckingham from Twitchen, was created in the late 1840s. Fields were cleared between a new farmstead and the combe.[149]

In 1851, excluding the 22 farms in Exmoor district, there were 225 in southern Exmoor of which 50 were under 50 acres, some

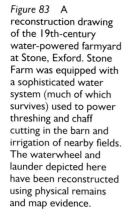

Figure 83 A reconstruction drawing of the 19th-century water-powered farmyard at Stone, Exford. Stone Farm was equipped with a sophisticated water system (much of which survives) used to power threshing and chaff cutting in the barn and irrigation of nearby fields. The waterwheel and launder depicted here have been reconstructed using physical remains and map evidence.

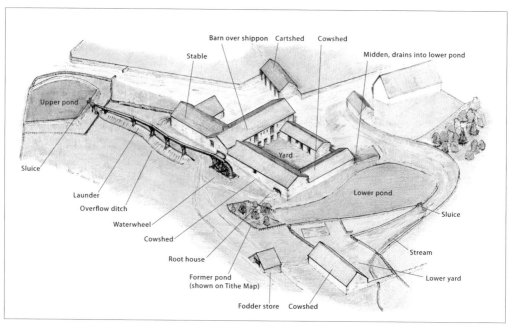

Figure 84
Reconstruction of
Lyshwell farmyard,
Molland, near the county
boundary at Hawkridge.
Situated below the
crest of a ridge, the
farmstead is afforded
some protection from
Exmoor's harsh climate
and relied on horse rather
than water power to
provide drive to the barn
adjoining the farmhouse.
The Buckingham family
worked Lyshwell and
neighbouring Landcombe
farms, rearing livestock
until the 1900s when
Landcombe farmstead
was abandoned.

worked part-time. Only Wellshead in Exford was over 500 acres
but there were farmsteads over 300 acres in Brushford, Dulverton
and Molland. Devon farms were smaller than Somerset ones: half
the farms in West Anstey were under 50 acres. Some of the farms
had fallen into disuse, but these were usually occupied by labouring
families or farmers out of business.

Dulverton farms had resident waggoners and the largest farm in
Twitchen had a resident waggoner and a shepherd. In Withypool,
with its poor communications, several farmers had resident errand
boys and girls, and cow boys were recorded at Exford. Many farms
also had three or more labourers living in. Children were often
excluded from the count, perhaps because they were unpaid, even
though they worked as house or farm servants. Many households
had lodgers, and overnight visitors were common, presumably due
to the difficulty of making a return journey in a day on Exmoor.
Older servants lived with their employers into old age.

Many farmsteads housed large families, some with as many
as 10 children spanning different age groups, grandchildren, in-
laws, cousins, nieces and nephews, and servants, all living under
the same roof. The largest households were in Brushford and 21
farms in the Somerset parishes had 10-17 residents. The eldest
son inherited the farm and was expected to house his siblings,
who often had no income. Adult children worked as labourers on

their parents' or brothers' farm until they died, so there were often middle-aged and even elderly unmarried children living in the farmhouses with wider family. At Edbrooke, Winsford, five children aged 28 to 45 worked the farm for their widowed father, while at Bickingcott in Twitchen an elderly farmer employed his children and grandchildren as servants. Such practices allowed family farms to remain undivided but sometimes resulted in personal tragedies such as illegitimate children and suicide.[150]

The 1866 Somerset agricultural returns show a sharp reduction in arable in most parishes after the 1840s except Brushford, Dulverton and Winsford, which produced grains, potatoes and turnips, the latter essential for fattening sheep. Enclosure of Hawkridge and Withypool commons provided winter employment and Withypool had four separate 'harvests' which employed everyone: turf, whortleberries, corn, and hay.[151]

By 1881 there were only 117 farms across the seven Somerset parishes and in Devon, Burch Farm (Twitchen – 600 acres) was the only farm over 500 acres. It was worked by ten men and four boys, who lived in the house with the family of five, a dairymaid, a housemaid, and a governess. In Brushford and Withypool, farms between 150 and 300 acres had increased at the expense of smaller ones but in Exford, Hawkridge, and Winsford farms up to 300 acres had been lost and a number of very large farms had been created, notably South Court (900 acres), Wellshead (800 acres) and Stone (800 acres). The smallest holdings survived in all parishes. Resident labourers were mainly young boys or widowers, and although there were fewer over all, Winsford had more than other parishes. Few Devon farms employed outside labour.[152]

At the end of the 19th century cattle herds increased in Brushford and Dulverton, possibly because of the nearby railway and cattle market, but in Hawkridge, Winsford and Withypool livestock numbers declined, perhaps because of feed and transport costs. Refrigerated ships brought beef and lamb from the southern hemisphere and Exmoor had to compete on quality. This could be why the Exmoor Horn Sheep Breeders' Society was formed in 1906. It held its first sale and show at Winsford in 1907, where 1,200 ewes were sold. By 1908 its flock book shows that the society had 132 members and had branded 25,000 pure Exmoor Horn sheep.

There had also been an increase in grassland, arable and wooded areas, especially at Withypool, probably representing improvements to the common since 1840. By 1905 there was twice as much arable at Exford as in 1801 and 50 per cent more at Hawkridge, and rough heath had increased between 1896 and 1906 in five of the Somerset parishes. Southern Exmoor was still well wooded with over 1,000 acres of woods and plantations in Dulverton parish.[153]

VILLAGE LIFE

Oldways End, on the boundary of Brushford and East Anstey, was developed after 1835 and by 1905 had a Methodist chapel (1845), a smithy, a carpenter's shop and sawpit, and a shop. Many other Exmoor villages acquired shops, post offices, chapels, and schools and these provided some employment for women and skilled men. Families combined trades to maximise income, such as one family in Molland in 1851, in which a thatcher was married to a baker, and the niece and nephew who lived with them worked as a dressmaker and schoolmaster respectively.

Options for women looking for work in a village were limited but employment was available. Labouring in the fields was one possibility, as in Winsford, where the corn, hay and potato crops required women workers. Indeed, some farmers would not rent a cottage to a labourer unless his wife worked in the fields, but as women received only 4s. for a six-day week working nine hours a day picking stones, weeding, and pulling turnips, they were often reluctant. They could make more by taking in washing. Another possibility was dairying, but women were not given work with livestock. Whatever the nature of the work, getting it was the important thing: a Dulverton doctor noted in 1867 that where women had work their families were better off and better housed.[154]

Work could also be difficult to come by for men and outside agriculture opportunities in road-mending, quarrying or mining were often casual or short-lived. In Devon between 1871 and 1891 employment on farms fell by over a quarter. Wages were also variable, especially in winter when there was less money to be

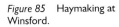

Figure 85   Haymaking at Winsford.

Population and Migration: 1841-1901

Differing dates of migration and ages of migrants may explain why the populations of Exford and Winsford peaked a decade earlier than average and those of Exmoor, West Anstey, and Twitchen peaked in 1871. Brushford's population did not decline and East Anstey's only slightly, partly due to the railway's arrival in 1873. Dulverton's population recovered between 1891 and 1901 but Molland lost a third of its inhabitants, probably including 30 mining families.

Advertisements and news from migrants probably encouraged emigration. In 1851 there were only 13 Dulverton people in Wales, mainly wives and servants, but by 1891 there were 102. In 1871 there were only seven Winsford and 90 Dulverton people in London but by 1891 there were 25 and 120 respectively. In 1881 two Withypool men were neighbours in Clase, Swansea, and nearby was a man from Twitchen. Two families from Withypool lived on the same street in Camberwell, shopkeeping and decorating. Dulverton migrants went to London (120), South Wales (102), Birmingham, Lancashire, and Middlesex before 1881.

Hawkridge people had not moved more than a few miles in 1851 but by 1891 of 93 people in England born in the parish 42 still lived there, 33 were in nearby parishes, and 18 were in London, Kent, and Essex. Most southern Exmoor people migrated as craftsmen, servants, or through marriage. Thomas Heal and William Mead of Winsford, carpenters, arrived by different routes at St Pancras, London in the early 1870s. A young brother and sister from Dulverton made and sold boots in Heath St., Birmingham in 1891.

Migrants to South Wales often boarded with people from their own parish. This led to concentrations of people from Dulverton and Winsford in Ystradyfodwyg, from Molland in Llandyfodwyg, both in Glamorgan,

Figure A   *The 1901 census for 16 Avon Hill Terrace, Glyncorrwg, Glamorgan, home of the Buckinghams from Twitchen and John Sanders from Higher Ball.*

Figure B *Memorial to the Pincombe family, would-be emigrants, in Molland churchyard. Thomas Pincombe, a Molland wheelwright, his wife and six children sailed from Plymouth in 1855 on an emigrant ship to Quebec, which foundered off the Cornish coast.*

Figure C *Memorial in Molland to Frances Dovell daughter of Henry Quartley and her son William who were drowned on a passage to the West Indies.*

and from Withypool and Exford in Mynyddyslwyn, Monmouthshire. From the 1880s migrants came to work in the coalmines but earlier they came as bootmakers, building workers, ostlers, gardeners, painters and decorators. Exmoor men settled at Cadoxton, Glamorgan as shoemakers and labourers.

John Winter, an Ebbw Vale coal heaver, moved from the Exmoor area c.1890 with his wife and nine children. William Buckingham, a Twitchen saddler, and his wife Bessie moved to Glyncorrwg c.1898 with their infant son. Of their five lodgers, all colliers and stablemen, four were from Twitchen.

Figure 86 Newland quarry, Exford. John Clarke bought the business in the 1870s and used his own boat to bring culm from South Wales via Porlock Weir to operate his three limekilns. Water wheels were used for pumping and raising stone with a winding engine.

earned unless there was work clearing the new enclosures. In 1867 carters had 9s. and labourers had 8s. a week, plus a cottage, cider, and other 'privileges'. But farmers claimed they would prefer to pay labourers 12s. or 13s. a week in cash. By the 1870s the standard wage for male agricultural labourers was between 11s. and 13s. a week, out of which rent and food had to be found. Stockmen earned up to 14s. and usually had a cottage, while living-in labourers earned £12 to £20 a year with board and food, which meant they were often better off.[155]

The quarries, which still produced stone for a lot of buildings on Exmoor, even though it was now possible to ship in brick and Welsh slate, provided some employment. Newland quarry in Exford's South Common, for instance, which was developed in response to the demand for lime for building and agriculture, especially from the Knights, was run by limeburners assisted by casual labour. One of the men was said in 1870 to have died after falling into the kiln. The lime, which rapidly absorbed his body, was used to plaster Withypool Methodist chapel. The quarry closed in 1914.[156]

Mining

Work was also to be found for a while in mining, specifically copper, until about 1900. Devon and Somerset were both significant producers, with the mine at Molland in operation from around 1845 until the 1870s when it switched to iron ore production. The Wheal Maria, later Eliza, on the river Barle, south-west of Simonsbath, opened as a copper mine in 1845, and in 1851 employed nine miners, six of whom lived in the adjoining cottage. The mine produced little copper or iron and closed in about 1857. It became notorious in 1858 when widower William Burgess murdered his young daughter, Anna, to save for drink the 2s. 6d. he paid for her keep at Simonsbath. He dumped her body in the shaft.[157]

The success of the nearby Brendon Hill iron mines led to a revival of iron mining in Exmoor, but although the thin lodes were often of high quality, they only produced small quantities of iron. Bremley averaged 3,500 tons of iron ore a year between 1871 and 1888 from six adits (drift mines) and in 1891, when over 4,000 tons was raised, around thirty men were employed, although only 11 were described as miners. The mines closed in 1893 and men returned to farm work or moved to the south Wales coalfields. Iron from Devon and Somerset was less than one per cent of national production at this time.[158]

The mining industry was small, so there was little dedicated provision needed for workers. For example, small iron mines at Twitchen and Exford worked in the 1860s and 1870s used existing labour and housing, while at Bremley a counting house was the only building provided. Only in Exmoor parish was it necessary to create housing for miners, where the Dowlais Iron Company built cottages for workers at the mines in Hangley Cleave, Cornham Ford and Blue Gate, east of Simonsbath, in the 1850s.[159]

Morgan Morgans of the Brendon Hill mines tried to reopen lead mines around Dulverton and, more successfully, iron mines on Eisen Hill in Winsford, which produced 7,000 tons a year in the 1860s. The ore was shipped from Minehead harbour (later from

Figure 87 At Cornham Ford in 1858 six cottages were built for miners with an office for the Dowlais Iron Company, seen on the left. Note the peat stacks. The mines closed and in 1871 all six cottages were uninhabited and later fell into ruin.

The Exmoor Cottages with three bed-rooms—cost of each 60*l.*

Figure 88 Blue Gate mine, with portable engine pumping, Exmoor, 1913. New shafts were sunk in 1910 and produced 1,700 tons of iron-rich ore, but closed in 1914. Mining was attempted elsewhere in the parish in the late 1850s and from 1910 to 1914.

Watchet via Gupworthy station on the Brendons) and cottages, an office, and a powder magazine were built across the Quarme in Exton. The men working at the mines are likely to have come from Winsford and North Molton, since two men who were killed in the mines were buried in Winsford. The venture foundered when the ore, which was in any case high in phosphorous, ran low and work stopped in 1877.

Iron mining also took place at Blackland in Withypool from 1875-81 and in 1895, with works run by the Ebbw Vale Company. The adits had tramways and an incline to a loading bay near the road. In 1907 the Withypool Mining Company tried to revive the business by sending ore previously mined and left in heaps to Minehead by traction engine, but without success. The Second World War revived interest but the ore was of poor quality.[160]

Poverty

The bad winter of 1848 led to high levels of unemployment, although some Exford labourers were put to work building roads on newly-enclosed commons. Unemployment in turn led to poverty and in 1851, 12 Winsford labourers and a handloom weaver were described as paupers. The parish could help by paying for a doctor to attend sick paupers and for funerals, and there were a few small charities and some Friendly Societies, but it was necessary to subscribe to the latter. Poverty was accompanied by overcrowding, and this meant that contagious diseases, such as diphtheria, which killed 11 children in Winsford in 1859, were more easily spread. In such conditions labourers' daughters and widows were vulnerable and illegitimate births were common, with girls often having to go into service, leaving their babies with their parents. By 1867 cottages in Exford had been improved and houses at Winsford and Hawkridge were good, with gardens and allotments, but Withypool was 'very wretched'.[161]

William Bradley, the relieving officer of Dulverton Union, had the job of paying the poor, visiting the sick and registering births and deaths. At this time paupers, who might be bedridden, weak, wounded, rheumatic or consumptive, could claim basic support from the parish, but as soon as they were judged able to work they had their pay stopped. This made the relieving officer's job a dangerous one, since those denied relief might be aggressive and some of the sick were infectious. From the diary he kept of his travels between villages in 1869-71 we know that he visited the Hawkridge postman who had injured his foot in a fall and Sarah Wynn of Brushford, aged 85, who had fallen and cut her face. Bradley got her a nurse but she died a week later. He was not an uncaring man, as he would get a doctor or nurse in when necessary, and was shocked to find a woman at Upton 'in great want and wretchedness and living all alone.'[162]

Children were expected to go out to work from the age of 11, and many from pauper families had to support their parents by

Figure 89   Improved 19th-century estate housing at Battleton, Dulverton. In 1867 a cottage in Dulverton cost up to £4 a year and many were small with only one bedroom. Lord Carnarvon and Sir Thomas Acland began building new houses on their estates during this period.

Figure 90 Exmoor House, now the headquarters of the Exmoor National Park Authority, was formerly the Dulverton workhouse, built in 1855. In 1861, 21 of 50 inmates came from Dulverton and in 1881 there were 46 inmates, and six Dulverton-born paupers were in workhouses as far away as Bethnal Green. By 1901 Dulverton had only 29 inmates, four of whom were vagrants.

working as servants on farms, where they would be contracted out for a year at 6d. or 1s. a week. In 1892 the Molland vestry claimed that this tradition encouraged boys to leave the area.

Another way to handle the poor was to send them to the workhouse. Stories such as *Oliver Twist* and *Christmas Day in the Workhouse*, which describe the practice of splitting couples and families between male and female wards, and the miserable 'dietaries' of bread and gruel, have given the Union workhouse a bad name, but many rural workhouses were attractively situated with gardens producing fresh food. People moved freely in and out of Dulverton workhouse, sometimes several times a year, like William Hayes of Winsford, who was disabled. Women could go in to have a child, usually illegitimate, and then leave, like Ann Lyddon from Dulverton, who brought six illegitimate children into the workhouse with her. After her confinement they left. Jane Morley of Dulverton brought three children into the house for a month when her husband deserted her. The workhouse was often the last resort of the disabled and mentally ill, like the young woman from Dulverton and the brother and sister from West Anstey, who were housed in South Molton workhouse in 1881. South Molton, which had modern sanitary arrangements and where the baths were 'all that could be desired' was still housing 'mental defective patients' in 1917.[163]

Between 1866 and 1927 many children were born in the workhouse, especially at the beginning and end of the period. Some women had several children there but only one stillbirth was recorded. Of those who died in the workhouse between 1866 and

1924 from the six southern Exmoor parishes 93 out of 136 were from Dulverton and 80 of the 93 were male. The only age group in which female deaths outnumbered male was in adults under 50, of whom 26 out of 36 were women. This is possibly due to the relatively high numbers of women who died in childbirth. Sarah Jane Perrott, aged 22, died the day after giving birth. Her baby died the following day and they were buried in a single coffin.[164]

In 1901 the declining population is reflected in smaller households. Withypool had the lowest average at 3.7 people per household, and 12 empty houses. Cottages with only two to four rooms housed families of up to twelve. At East Anstey, Brushford, Hawkridge, Winsford and Twitchen a third or more of dwellings had fewer than five rooms and at Molland it was nearly half. In Twitchen a family of five occupied a two-roomed dwelling and at least one other child lived out. By contrast Withypool had only four small cottages and Exmoor only one.[165]

The tough life on the moor and the hardships of the poor probably influenced Ernest Bevin, Minister of Labour during the Second World War. He was born in Winsford in 1881, the seventh child of Diana Tudball, whose husband William Bevin disappeared in the 1870s. Diana lived with butcher William Pearce but surnamed all her children Bevin. She worked as a servant, midwife, laundress, and occasional barmaid and died in 1889 aged only 48. Ernest attended both church school and Wesleyan Sunday school and after his mother's death he lived with his brother-in-law, a railway porter, in Devon. One brother went to an uncle in Bristol and another went to Ashway, Dulverton, as a farm servant. Coincidentally, Ashway was the birthplace in 1821 of Sir George Williams, founder of the YMCA.[166]

Educational provision for the poor greatly increased in the later 19th century. Several parishes provided day schools for the poor and there were charity schools at Dulverton and Brushford, church and chapel Sunday schools, and a few dame schools in which a woman would teach two or three infants to read. Farmers complained about boys being kept at school and in parishes like Winsford where education was available to labouring families many boys eventually left to look for better work. By 1902 every parish in southern Exmoor had a school, mostly built following the Education Acts of 1870 and 1876, which introduced compulsory education for all children.[167]

Figure 91   Exford school, still held in the 1873 school and teacher's house, on the left, and sympathetic addition right. In 1902 there were 74 children on the register in three classes and attendance was good.

Religion

After early difficulties Methodism found a firm foothold on Exmoor by appealing to independent farmers, craftsmen, miners,

Figure 92   Molland band
around 1900. Many
churches replaced viols
and bassoons with organs
or harmoniums. The
Molland church band
accompanied the organ
when it was installed
in 1877 but thereafter
may have had to confine
themselves to secular
occasions. Dulverton had
a silver band in the late
19th century.

and labourers. Its lay preachers, such as the Molland labourer
who was preaching in 1881, were also able to take advantage of
the fact that many isolated Exmoor churches had few services.
There were Methodist chapels or meeting rooms at Twitchen,
Oldways end, and two in Molland. The Bible Christians were
very successful in the Brendons and on Exmoor, although many
chapels, such as the one in Winsford, later became Wesleyan
Methodist. A Bible Christian chapel was built in 1902 at
Dulverton where there was also a well-established Congregational
chapel. In 1910 there were regular services at Methodist chapels
in Exford, Winsford and Withypool.[168]

The established church also enjoyed a resurgence of confidence.
Many churches were largely rebuilt at this period, notably

Dulverton in 1852-5, East Anstey in 1871 and Withypool in 1901. Others were restored including Winsford, where the architect, John Dando Sedding, died in 1891 while working on the church.[169]

THE COMING OF THE RAILWAY

The Devon and Somerset railway from Taunton to Barnstaple, first planned in 1845, opened between Wiveliscombe and Barnstaple in 1873. It was a single-track, broad-gauge line and it was operated from 1876 by the Great Western Railway. Dulverton, the most important intermediate station, became the terminus for the Exe

Figure 93 Track of Exmoor to Porlock railway near Larkbarrow, seen running diagonally from left of photograph. In the 1850s Frederic Knight began his mineral line across Exmoor parish to Porlock but the iron ore was insufficient to meet the expense so the scheme was abandoned.

Figure 94 Probably the first train in to South Molton station in 1873 on the Devon and Somerset railway. The line also included stations in Brushford, named Dulverton, East Anstey, and Molland, later known as Bishop's Nympton and Molland. There were seven trains each way by the 1890s.

Valley line from Tiverton and Exeter in 1885. By 1881 the railway employed a station master and 10 other staff in Brushford and Dulverton, a station master at East Anstey and 10 workers in East and West Anstey and Molland.[170]

The coming of the railway had a profound impact on agriculture. When in 1873 the earl of Carnarvon opened a toll-free monthly cattle market near Dulverton station, cattle trucks could carry livestock by rail to new owners or to slaughter within hours. Sheep could be brought by rail to Winsford's new fair and large flocks could be transported to London once they had been slaughtered. When rinderpest wiped out most of London's cows in 1865-6 the capital was able to import milk by rail, much of it from Exmoor, Brushford and Dulverton dairy herds, which had increased by 50 per cent between 1876 and 1896. Hundreds of tons of fertiliser were brought up the line in spring enabling farmers to increase production while the same trains took their produce to more lucrative markets. The daily rabbit train from South Molton, which ran until the mid-20th century, supplied London poulterers. In 1903, 750 trucks of livestock were dispatched from Molland, East Anstey and Dulverton besides over 19,000 tons of freight and 27,000 parcels.[171]

The railways also boosted tourism. Lord Carnarvon built the *Carnarvon Arms* hotel beside Dulverton station for visitors coming to hunt, shoot and fish on Exmoor, and the poet Tennyson stayed there in 1891. Most visitors were anglers, as hotel guests were allowed to fish freely on Lord Carnarvon's stretches of the Barle and Exe. The GWR subsidised horse-drawn passenger services from Dulverton station to Minehead, Lynton and Lynmouth during the summer from the 1890s and the Spencer brothers hired out cars to those who could afford four guineas a day. They also had one of the area's first telephones. Other Dulverton businesses supplied tourists with ammunition, clothing, fishing equipment, and 'pictorial postcards' and the town's laundry offered hand-powered washing with no unpleasant chemicals. It was said that, in 1900, 50 people in Dulverton tailored riding habits and country clothing for visitors and their servants.[172]

The *Lion Hotel*, Dulverton, with 16 beds and stabling for 35 horses in 1888, accommodated families, some of whom returned each year to hunt and fish. One visitor in 1908 objected to the animal cruelty enjoyed by fellow guests. Some guests studied the flora and fauna, painted, or walked from Simonsbath or Lynton, following the *Lorna Doone* trail. Farmers and cottagers offered teas with home-made clotted cream and drove visitors to and from Dulverton station by pony trap.[173]

The railway also brought employment: by 1903 the Dulverton station staff numbered 15, there were seven at East Anstey and three at Molland. But although the railways had assisted emigration, encouraged tourism, and brought cheaper supplies of coal, fertilisers, seeds, and building materials, they went into decline in Exmoor in the 1930s. Passenger numbers fell and the quantity of freight carried was reduced, partly due to the remoteness of stations from the communities they served. The local lines closed in the 1960s.[174]

The years before the First World War are often seen as a golden age, with improvements in education, welfare, health and sanitation, although Exmoor often lagged behind. Many enjoyed a better standard of living, could travel for pleasure or migrate for work. There were more social facilities, a local police force, and increasing democracy as the old vestries gave way to parish and rural district councils. Many women were able to hold local office and there had been several extensions to male suffrage. By 1910 Exmoor was a parish with a small village at Simonsbath. Tourism was bringing revenue to the area and hotels were built to cater for visitors. For the area as a whole the great investment in high farming did not pay off. It was tourism that would eventually cushion the area from the declining profitability of hill farming.[175]

Exmoor in Living Memory

Figure 95 The last train on the Taunton to Barnstaple line, October 1966. The loss of the railway and the increasing dependence on motor transport have changed the social structure of many settlements as well as having an impact on the environment.

The 20th century brought enormous changes to Exmoor. The loss of traditional mixed farming, the introduction of the tractor and other machinery, the influence of different government policies, entry into the European common market, and subsidies, have resulted in the redundancy of traditional buildings and alterations to the landscape. Villages have diversified from supporting the farming community into providing homes for the wealthy retired, commuters and enterprising craftspeople, and accommodation and services for tourists and weekenders. Although this has brought revenue and even capital to Exmoor it is said to have pushed house prices beyond the reach of those born in the area.

Two world wars, the spread of electricity, telephones, radio, and television, and an influx of new permanent and temporary residents have brought Exmoor out of its relative isolation. Road access is still poor and the loss of the railway impacted on some businesses, but one or two manufacturers have established themselves in Dulverton. Severe weather can still disrupt life but snowploughs, helicopters, and communication technology ensure that no-one is beyond help. The creation of the Exmoor National Park raised the profile of the area and several local societies, notably the Exmoor Society, emerged to protect the landscape, flora and fauna, as well as the villages and built environment.

FARMING THE LAND

In 1929 F.G. Smyth-Richards succeeded his father as land agent to the Exmoor estate (25,000 acres). Farms, previously in hand, were let to former estate labourers and shepherds who knew how to make the moor pay. The estate still managed seven herdings of around a thousand acres each and grazed around five hundred Cheviot ewes. Each flock was tended by a shepherd who used an Exmoor pony to cover the area. Lambs were wintered at Castle Hill, Devon, and wethers were sold at Bridgwater fair, but after 1937 extensive breaking and re-seeding of the old grassland ensured that the flock could be over wintered on the moor. In the 1930s Galloway cattle were introduced to the moor; previously Irish shorthorn yearlings had been bought in and sold in the autumn when in calf. Road improvements made carting of fodder

Figure 96 Making
farming pay, the
Buckingham family
haymaking at Pinkery.
Small farmers survived
by using family labour
with almost no
investment in machinery
or improvement. The
Buckingham family
were typical, facing
poor conditions and
lacking capital.

and moving of stock easier but required extensive fencing to
prevent stock wandering.[176]

Farm size reached a temporary limit in the late 19th century.
Taking in extra land often meant high costs but low returns as
labour became more expensive and prices fell. Some farms created
by amalgamation were divided, and by 1939 the number of farms
over 150 acres had fallen overall. Twitchen had no farms over 150
acres, compared with five in 1916. Between 1916 and 1936 herds
and flocks declined, especially in Dulverton, Exmoor and Winsford,
where the number of cattle fell by a quarter. There was a similar
reduction in sheep in Dulverton and Winsford but at Twitchen
stock increased. More pigs were kept and the Devon parishes had
large flocks of poultry. East Anstey and Molland had small acreages
of soft fruit.

Hill farming was said to be dying out in the 1930s, with many
farmers forced to live on credit and bills inherited along with
farms. This was blamed on a flood of cheap refrigerated imports.
Farmers replaced leys with permanent pasture, but they often
reverted to rush and bracken because they were no longer limed or
slagged to counter the soil acidity.[177]

Some owners thought farming was still a good investment.
Farms rebuilt in early 20th century include Kennels and Hinam
farms, Dulverton and Worth, Winsford. The Rev. Sweetapple
Horlock established a hostel for urban boys to learn farm work
at Tarr Steps Farm (100 acres) in 1926 and served teas to visitors.
Somerset County Council organised buttermaking classes on farms
around Dulverton.[178]

In 1927 the industrialist Sir Robert Waley Cohen purchased
1,745 acres including Honeymead Farm (916 acres) in Exmoor
parish from Lord Fortescue. He spent most weekends there and
served on the Rural District Council. He kept dairy cattle and a
prize-winning flock of Exmoor sheep, made 75 acres of hay, grew
potatoes, oats, turnips and rape, and was noted for paying good
wages. The outbreak of war helped to make the estate profitable.
The heather moor was ploughed for corn and potatoes, and
Friesian cows bought at Reading were housed in concrete and
asbestos shippons built in 1940-1. Indeed, Honeymead Farm
was one of the few in Exmoor to be A-rated in 1941, supporting
94 cattle, 1,123 sheep, 37 pigs and 176 poultry. There were also a
tractor, seven engines in the yard and six working horses. In 1944
Sir Robert paid £1,400 for a bull to improve the dairy herd and
by 1967 he had 319 pedigree Devon cattle including six bulls.
He bought a lorry, and introduced machinery such as a powered
binder for cutting corn, for which he employed a farm mechanic.
From 1941 to 1965 two waterwheels generated electricity.[179]

The 1941 farm survey for the area makes depressing reading for several Somerset parishes. Although almost all farms in the Ansteys, Molland and Twitchen and most in Brushford and Dulverton were A-rated, elsewhere many were graded C. Surveyors may have assessed farms differently but the fact is that many Exmoor farms were poorly or badly managed by farmers who were elderly, in poor health, and lacking in ambition, capital and labour. One tenant of Oak, East Anstey, was found to have derelict fields, where no fertilizer had been used, and was turned off the land for bad farming. Another case in point is Slade Farm (180 acres) in Dulverton, which was managed for an absent farmer by a bailiff who had to cultivate 43 acres of arable crops and look after 31 cattle, while lacking labour, horses and implements. Small Devon farms rarely employed anyone outside the family, and several, especially in Exford, still used waterpower. Many used pairs of working horses instead of tractors, even though several had petrol engines in the yard. Some farmers did not even own horses. However, there were success stories. Zeal Farm in Hawkridge still depended on a 10-horse power water wheel and 24 working horses but was A-rated and had a tractor. Neighbouring East Shercombe was being improved by a new tenant using a tractor and Ashway Farm in Dulverton (400 acres) was being improved after long neglect. The 68 acres of arable, 51 cattle, 39 sheep, four pigs and 30 fowls, were managed with one labourer, a tractor, two horses and waterpower.[180]

Figure 97 Hawkridge wheelwright John Lock, still at work in his 70s in the 1930s.

Figure 98 Subsoiling at Blackpits, Exmoor, in 1952. The war had shown that Britain could feed itself and renewed enthusiasm for farming improvement. However, loss of wild moorland to farming was not welcomed by everyone as attitudes to the countryside changed.

After the War

Women formed around twelve per cent of the workforce in the Somerset parishes before and during the Second World War. By contrast, in Devon they formed 20 per cent of the workforce in 1946, by which time three Women's Land Army members remained and 31 prisoners of war worked on farms. Between 1936 and 1946 arable production rose by a third in Somerset and in 1966 Winsford still had 275 acres of arable, producing turnips and rape for fodder and 10 smallholdings. Arable production doubled in Devon, mainly due to increases in animal fodder and barley; the potato acreage also increased, from 28 to 161. In terms of livestock, pig production halved and dairying declined except in the Ansteys. By contrast, total cattle numbers rose by over a third between 1946 and 1986 and sheep flocks increased threefold to over 148,000. Poultry increased in Devon but halved in Somerset; in 1941 there were six specialist poultry farms in East and West Anstey and in 1946 the Ansteys, Twitchen and Molland had over 15,000 fowls. But by 1976 the only poultry farm was at Brushford with over 25,000 birds. Rough grazing, which had been increasing steadily since the late 19th century was reduced in the 1940s. The overall trend was towards improvement of the land and, in the 30 years to 1966, 5,000 acres in southern Exmoor were improved. Farm sizes reduced again post-war, so that Withypool, which had 18 farms in 1881, had 32 in 1966.[181]

Slade Farm, Dulverton was an example of post-war modernisation. In 1947 it was a stock-raising farm with a small house with no bathroom or kitchen, a one-up one-down cottage, and a threshing machine and shafting driven by an overshot water wheel. By 1951 it was one of the best farms in the district with two concrete cattle yards, a manure tank, a 60-foot lambing shed, and a 60-ton tower silo with electric power and light. The farm carried 70 Devon and Devon cross cattle, 250 sheep, 500 poultry and 18 pigs.

Other farms followed this example. By 1959 Pinkery Farm had a windmill-powered electric plant and Emmet's Grange had a modern shippon with concrete standings, automatic water bowls and electricity. The situation on the Exmoor estate did not seem as promising in 1950, when there was only one tractor and little fertiliser was used, but Galloway cows were soon being crossed with Hereford bulls to produce polled, white-faced cattle, and these commanded high prices. Cheviot ewes were crossed with Dorset, Leicester or Texel rams and grazing was supplemented with 5,200 tons of silage, 375 tons of hay and 120 acres of rape. Following the deaths of Lord and Lady Fortescue in 1958 many farms were sold to tenants but 9,600 acres remained and supported about 350 cattle and 4,000 sheep, rising to 8,000 in the summer of 1960. By 1980 over 2,000 acres was improved grass and the estate carried 784 Galloway and Galloway-cross cattle and 7,295 sheep. The farm bailiff employed seven shepherds, five tractor drivers, four stockmen, and a fencer.[182]

The railway assisted farming and facilitated events like the Somerset County Show, held near Dulverton in 1905, and Bampton fair. During the First World War ponies were taken by rail and sea to serve on the western front and in the early 20th century eggs and chickens were packed in Dulverton and taken by train to London. In 1933 over 600 cattle trucks left Dulverton, East Anstey and Molland stations and in 1954 a Westmorland farmer moved his stock, including pedigree Friesians, to Molland by train. But as road haulage became more common rail traffic declined and the Taunton to Barnstaple railway closed in 1964.[183]

In the later 20th century, orchards and working horses disappeared and large new covered yards were built. Modernisation continued, but many farms in Exmoor also went into decline. The cost of fuel and feed increased, and farmers had to subsidise their income with other employment or the

Figure 99 Airlifting hay to sheep on Exmoor in the severe winter of 1962-3. A helicopter ferried supplies from Dulverton station to outlying farms. Supplies brought by helicopter to Warren Farm, Exmoor, included hay for 900 sheep. The sheep walked to the farmstead along the tops of frozen hedges.

holiday trade. At least one turned to organic farming in the 1950s. Between 1966 and 1986 the number of smallholdings halved. Of 183 farms and smallholdings in the seven Somerset parishes 103 were worked part-time. This figure was even higher in East Anstey, where holdings were small: 20 out of 29 farms there were worked part-time. By the 1980s Horsen (748 acres) and Wintershead (300 acres) in Exmoor had only 85 acres of rough pasture to support 170 cows and 1,050 ewes. They also wintered 400 sheep and 300 bullocks with 40 acres of rape and turnips and about 240 acres of hay and silage. More outside labour was employed in 1986 than in 1966, which meant added costs. Some farmsteads were even abandoned in the 1970s (probably including Well, now in Withypool parish) and any put up for sale had to have good prospects for hunting and tourism. Between 1973 and 1988 in the national park cattle numbers fell from 55,000 to 45,000 and sheep increased from 350,000 to 500,000.

Some blame Exmoor farming's decline on the loss of the traditional moorland management skills developed by generations of people who were familiar with the landscape. Instead of improving the moorland, farmers have been favouring less intensive agriculture, and allowed stock levels to reduce, which some maintain has led to the encroachment of scrub and bracken onto the grazing. Livestock itself often consists of introduced breeds which do not necessarily thrive on Exmoor, unlike the Exmoor pony, the Exmoor Horn or Devon Closewool sheep, or the Ruby Red and South Devon cattle. The experimental husbandry farm at Liscombe, Dulverton, closed in 1989 to the disappointment of local farmers, causing such concern that in 1990 the Exmoor Society organised a Farming Conservation Conference at Dulverton.[184]

By the late 20th century hill farming was supported by subsidies and environmentally sensitive area payments. In 1992, Stone in Exford, a 1,568-acre sheep farm, derived over half its estimated £60,000 income from subsidies. In 2005 a 'typical' 800-acre hill farm of which 600 acres was moorland could support 600 sheep and 50 cattle, while a valley farm like Broford in Dulverton with over 400 acres of better land could support several hundred cattle. Two thirds of the income of the 'typical' hill farm would be subsidy, producing a profit of around £7,000 a year. Few farms have the capacity to overwinter young animals, which were sold in the nearby sheep market at Cutcombe or general markets like Taunton, until it closed in 2008.

Although there was no outbreak within the park itself, the foot and mouth epidemic of 2001 changed attitudes to farming. The way in which it took hold was attributed directly to industrialised agriculture and feed systems, and it led to a surge in interest among consumers in independent producers. This, coupled with the increasing concern for environmental damage and climate change, means Exmoor is having to come to terms with the conflict between making a living and farming sustainably in a sensitive area. The development of farmers' markets, support for local food shops, and the creation of niche markets for quality produce are one way to cope with this, and may lead to radically different ways of farming Exmoor in the 21st century.[185]

LIVING ON THE MOOR

Early 20th-century communities were self-sufficient. Each parish had a church and most had a school, a meeting room, a public house, a post office – which might be combined with a small shop – a blacksmith and a wheelwright or carpenter. There were sports clubs, bands, and church and chapel choirs. Exford and Winsford had shoemakers, dressmakers, tailors, saddlers and grocers, and Winsford also had an auctioneer and a police constable. In bad winters Exmoor Stores in Exford employed men who walked several miles carrying groceries such as dried fish to distant cottages. Sometimes individuals plied more than one trade, such as the Molland postmaster in 1935 who was a boot repairer, confectioner, newsagent and tobacconist, working in a parish which also had a grocer and baker, two blacksmiths, wheelwrights and an agricultural engineer. Dulverton supplied banks, surgeons, solicitors, coachbuilders, watchmakers, laundry, hairdressers, chemist, ironmonger, confectioner and cycle dealer.[186]

Figure 100 The 19th-century kitchen at Driver Farm, Exmoor in the 1920s. By 1959 the farmhouse had a bathroom and hot water but two labourer's cottages had bucket closets and shared well water.

Family Life

Figure 101 New local
authority housing planned
for Battleton, 1929, with
baths. Dulverton was short
of accommodation, too;
in 1934 a scheme was
drawn up to replace 55
unfit houses but only about
40 new three-bedroom
houses were planned.

Life, even in a large farmhouse, had its privations. Some had
no bathrooms and a seven-bedroom farmhouse at Winsford
shared a well with several cottages in 1926. At Exmoor, Horsen
and Emmet's Grange farmhouses had bathrooms and private
electric supplies but most cottages had only a bucket closet.
Electricity came to Simonsbath only in 1962, and before that a
man with a generator would charge wireless batteries for those
who had a radio. By 1969 new cottages had been built and others
refurbished with modern sanitation but still with private water
and electricity supplies. However, Driver and Hoaroak cottages

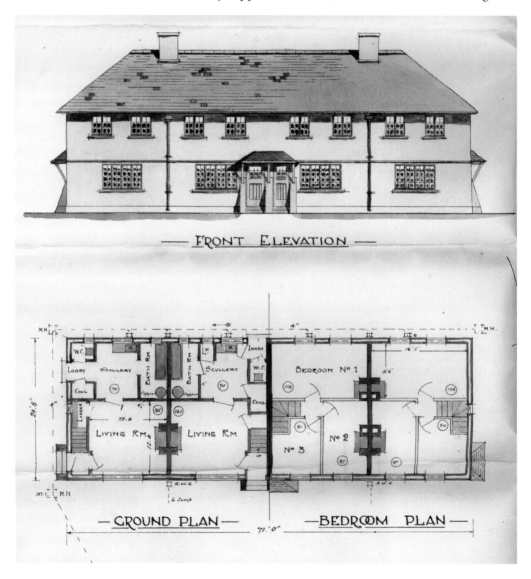

still lacked basic facilities. Paired workers' cottages were built between the wars and the first local authority houses were built in the late 1920s.[187]

Cottagers generally had a hard life, especially the women who brought up many children with little money and without running water or sanitation. Since farmers still gave cider to their workers some women also had to cope with husbands who drank, and work was insecure. Life in a cottage could still be overcrowded, as it must have been for the Winsford couple who had 15 children. Dulverton cottagers could take their Sunday dinner to be cooked in a baker's oven for 1d. but in the home open fires were still used for cooking and boiling clothes; although coal had been easily available since the opening of the railway, peat was used as fuel because it was 'free'. In Dulverton many relied on the river for water, but it was contaminated with sewage and blood and offal from slaughtering pigs and chickens.

Children were expected to fit in home and farm duties around school and to catch trout, eel, or rabbit, which was staple fare for poorer families until the 1950s. They collected whortleberries, wild strawberries, and cranberries, which were sold to raise money but vegetables and other fruit were grown at home. Some families kept a pig and poultry so eggs and milk came from their own stock or from neighbours. The more fortunate children rode to school, and schools like Simonsbath even had grazing for ponies, but most cottage children had to walk. A boy attending Twitchen school in the 1920s walked and ran three-and-a-half miles each way despite having a heart defect.

Country Houses

Country houses built or rebuilt in the late 19th and early 20th-centuries included Knapp in East Anstey, Hele Manor and The Claw in Brushford, Hollam, Northmoor House, Ashwick with its private theatre and New Invention in Dulverton. Easy rail access from London for people and commodities, cheap and plentiful coal, and enough servants made life reasonably comfortable and sociable. In the 1930s there were 18 indoor servants at Pixton Park, later reduced to eight: four gardeners, a carpenter and grooms. Unless the Herberts were at their villa in Portofino there would be guests or shooting parties most weekends. Hilaire Belloc was a regular visitor and once set his bed alight by smoking. The Fortescues had around 10 servants at Simonsbath House, a governess and tutor for the children, a car, and horses. They rode, hunted with friends or attended gymkhanas and country shows.[188]

Figure 102 Anti-hunt protesters in 1957. Hunting was still the main attraction of Exmoor for wealthy families and provided social events such as puppy shows, point to point (horse racing), and hunt balls. Farmers and cottagers hunted or followed the hunt according to their circumstances although not all local people approved.

War Time

During the Second World War casualties among local men who joined up were light. However, there were many air accidents in Exmoor, the first casualties of which were five crew of an Anson that crashed in Somerset in January 1940. That September a Wellington bomber crashed onto a cottage near Simonsbath and in September 1943 a B 17 Flying Fortress also crashed at Simonsbath. Exmoor, like Salisbury plain, lent itself to military training before and during the First World War, but the Second World War had the greatest physical impact when infantry and artillery training turned Exmoor into a battleground. The 1st Motor Battalion of the Grenadier Guards was based at Winsford in 1942, the Royal Observer Corps at East Anstey and Exford, and the Parachute Regiment at Exford in 1942 and Exmoor in 1945. There were a searchlight position, an anti-aircraft battery and a decoy on Exmoor, Royal Artillery ranges on Dunkery, and gunnery ranges and tank training on the coast. The noise of gunfire, shells and mortars must have been a constant background to life on the moor and made working with animals difficult.[189]

In 1944 several thousand American troops arrived at Dulverton station in preparation for D Day. On one day 15 troop trains arrived, each carrying 1,000 men and stores. There was a surprise visit by General Eisenhower, still remembered by local

Figure 103   War
Office map, 1941,
showing Tom's Hill
and Larkbarrow farms,
requisitioned for an
artillery range, in the
centre of the impact
area; blue enclosures
are gun areas. Exmoor
was extensively used for
military training. Antiquity
Stars on posts were used
to prevent archaeological
sites being targeted. One
survives at Alderman's
Barrow near Exford.

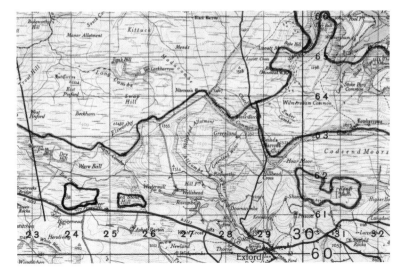

Figure 104   Larkbarrow
Farm site today, shell
holes still visible. It was
shelled to ruins, mainly by
American troops. The land
was managed as a herding
from Warren Farm but the
five square miles proved
hard to manage and were
peppered with unexploded
shells, which were not
removed until the 1960s.

people. He arrived at Dulverton station and rode a horse over the
moors to Winsford and Withypool, where he called at the *Royal
Oak* before returning to Dulverton. The Americans, unfamiliar
with English lanes, had several accidents, one of which saw them
drive a truck through the parapet of Dulverton bridge into the
river Barle.[190]

Local men joined the Local Defence Volunteers, later the
Minehead and 4th Devonshire battalions of the Home Guard.
They had rifle ranges and a large area for grenade practice

east of Stone Farm, Exford, and they clearly practised with explosives, since 56 Molotov Cocktails were uncovered at Exford in 1976. The Brushford platoon of the Dulverton Company was under actor and writer Ronald Pertwee, so it is perhaps no surprise that to raise money for the Red Cross the company put on entertainment.[191]

Civilians endured blackouts and rationing, although Exmoor's self sufficiency probably helped. Many people took houses or hotel rooms on Exmoor to escape the Blitz and Exford school accommodated 100 evacuees and two head teachers. In addition, child and adult evacuees were brought to Dulverton, where houses were requisitioned, including Ashwick and Hollam. The additional population in July 1940 was 856, more than half Dulverton's pre-war population. Local children had new friends to play with and the older girls found boyfriends and husbands among the soldiers. The evacuees who arrived were unused to much walking, so motor transport was arranged to take children to school in Simonsbath and that continued after the war. Road improvements were carried out, partly as relief work for the unemployed and by the 1930s three GWR lorries delivered heavy goods from Dulverton station to Exford, Winsford, Withypool and Simonsbath. There were also regular buses. Dulverton had a cinema, dances, concerts, and other entertainment, so perhaps it is little wonder that many young people are said to have enjoyed the war and found life dull afterwards. Even Simonsbath had a cinema and dances in a hut at Honeymead.[192]

Figure 105 The Home Guard on exercise, Exmoor, 1944. The Exmoor Company included cavalry and had platoons at Exford, Simonsbath, Winsford, and Withypool.

Figure 106 Dulverton in the wake of the 1952 flood. There were many stories of narrow escapes from drowning. At Dulverton the river Barle destroyed several buildings and people were rescued from bedroom windows.

The isolation of parishes like Exmoor must have been keenly felt after the war. In 1947 Simonsbath was five-and-a-half miles from a bus stop; Withypool had one bus to Minehead on Saturdays, weather permitting, and the postman had to bring chemist's supplies. Severe winters, such as Exmoor suffered in the 1960s and 1970s could cut off homes for weeks; in 1963 the snow was so high and hard that a pony could be ridden along the hedge tops. The August 1952 flood, which devastated Lynmouth, also damaged Exmoor, sweeping away most of the Tarr Steps clapper bridge. A wall of water carried timber through Exford and Winsford and floodwaters damaged the hotel at Simonsbath and premises in Withypool. Ten road bridges were destroyed or seriously damaged. Today, some Exmoor farms and houses still rely on spring water and electricity from a generator.

Modern Exmoor

In the late 20th century people who once travelled by pony trap or bus to Dulverton to shop went further afield by car, and village services declined. When asked if there were any problems the Winsford postmaster replied 'in this idyllic place! You must be joking!' However, another resident complained, 'there is very little left in the village to close down' – an unfortunate remark, as Winsford later fought in vain to keep its school. However, Dulverton's position as the local town had been strengthened first

Figure 107 Local authority housing beyond the bridge at Withypool. Most of southern Exmoor's native population has been lost. Retired farmers and labourers remain in the villages where they worked living in homes provided by the local authority but their children and grandchildren have often moved away.

in the 19th century by the siting there of the police station, fire brigade, and workhouse, and in the 20th century by the electricity company, the Park authority headquarters, the area's middle school, medical centre and dental surgery, and over 40 shops and services. With 1,486 residents in 2001 Dulverton accounted for over a third of southern Exmoor's population.[193]

With social housing in short supply, another perceived threat was the number of second homes in Exmoor. Often owned by well-off individuals or families based in London and empty for much of the year, they were seen as undermining local services and reducing the resident population whose incomes are sometimes less than half the national average. Yet without incomers settlements would die: the population of the area was 3,896 in 2001, 1,055 less than in 1851. Employment in agriculture is also harder to come by; at Molland the numbers working in the sector fell from 182 in 1926 to 52 in 1986.[194]

By the beginning of the 21st century communications and services have reached most households and life on the moor has changed. Villages have a church but neither a service every Sunday nor resident clergy, and most have a village hall, mobile library service, and local societies and clubs, such as the Winsford Exmoor Community Computer Centre. Winsford and Molland each have a cricket team, although Molland's has to play away in the early season because cattle graze the outfield. Only Dulverton, East Anstey, and Exford retain their schools and many nonconformist chapels have closed. Some villages have lost their

Figure 108 Population maps, 1851 and 2001. These show density as acres per person because the popultion density is so low. The four Devon parishes lost 48 per cent of their population. Molland and Twitchen lost two thirds, half between 1871 and 1931. Brushford's population rose by nearly two thirds. Its position outside the national park but close to Dulverton has encouraged 20th-century development.

shops and post offices and those that survive, along with cafes, and public houses, such as those at Exford, do so only because of the tourist season. Dulverton, Dunster and South Molton still provide shops and services but increasingly people shop in Taunton, Exeter, and Barnstaple.

PROTECTING EXMOOR

The creation of Exmoor National Park and, shortly afterwards, the pressure group The Exmoor Society, reflected national trends over the protection of the rural landscape. Intense local debate about the potential impact of farming and forestry proposals played a significant role in shaping national policy for the countryside and, in particular, led to the development of the management agreement approach and modern agri-environment schemes as well as helping formulate the policy for afforestation in the uplands. In a real sense, what happened on Exmoor made national policy.

National Parks Movement

The American concept of 'setting aside' spectacular landscapes, which began in the second half of the 19th century, was influential in creating the National Parks movement, as was an awareness of the need for areas for recreation close to towns, a growing appreciation of ecology and the general loss of rural character and ways of life through the 1930s and 1940s. This inspired the fondness – sometimes bordering on rampant nostalgia – for rural life and landscape which found widespread expression in such books as Dorothy Hartley's *The Countryman's England* (1935) or Stanley Baron's *Westward Ho! From Cambria to Cornwall!* (1934): 'All day long I travelled over the moor and its subsidiary hills, first by a well tarred road, then a bridleway which petered out in heather; to Withypool; to a Dulverton chemist's for my paper; to the valley of the Haddeo (where cars, in the name of all things good, are forbidden).'[195]

In 1931 the Addison Committee reported on the feasibility of National Parks and the improvement of facilities for countryside recreation. Then, a mass trespass on Kinder Scout in 1932 raised the national debate on the value of wild open spaces that were in private ownership. In 1942 the Scott Report, *Land Utilisation in Rural Areas*, saw 'the establishment of National Parks in Britain as long overdue' and by the time of the later Dower Report on National Parks in England and Wales it was assumed that the case had been made. Dower defined a National Park as 'an extensive area of beautiful and relatively wild country in which: the characteristic landscape beauty is strictly preserved, access and facilities for public open-air enjoyment are amply provided, wildlife and buildings and places of architectural and historic interest are suitably protected, while established farming use is effectively maintained.'

The 1947 Hobhouse Report considered potential National Parks and defined their 'special qualities'. Exmoor was, for the first time, explicitly identified. The National Park was designated in 1954, the eighth of the original 10 National Parks, and at 69,280 hectares, one of the smallest. At the time, Exmoor was described as 'a potential National Park which is happily free from problems'. However, the proposal was met with fierce local opposition, especially from the County Councils. That resulted in the National Park being much smaller than originally envisaged (initially the National Park was to include the Quantock Hills). The fact that it was designated at all is due largely to the actions of pressure groups, which rallied in support of the designation.

Exmoor was included in the original list because of its spectacular coastline, 'fine heather, bracken and grass moorland'

Figure 109 The Chains, the bleak moorland ridge that runs through the central part of western Exmoor. Afforestation proposals aroused strong opposition. Namely articles in the local and national press saying that conifers had no place in National Parks, which had been created because of aesthetic considerations.

and 'beautiful wooded valleys'. The overall intimate character of this soft upland with its 'mosaic of contrasts' in a relatively limited area made it unique among National Parks. The report highlighted 'antiquities in great profusion on Exmoor, including stone-circles, barrows, hut circles as well as earthworks'. Despite this, it was not until 1995 that the Environment Act included 'cultural heritage' explicitly as one of the National Parks' purposes in respect of conservation and enhancement.

The Exmoor Society

In 1958 Lord Fortescue, whose estate included much of the former Royal Forest, put forward a proposal to plant conifers on large areas of The Chains. This reflected a national drive to expand the area of English forest, although some consider that the initiative was a direct response to the Lynmouth Flood Disaster and was an attempt to hold water in the upland. Dr Richard Harper of Barnstaple organised a petition against what he saw as the desecration of this hitherto unspoilt moorland. On 4 June 1958 the Devon Committee of the National Park issued a press release stating that it was in deadlock over the afforestation proposal. Later, in June, a meeting was held on The Chains itself, with Lord Strang (Chairman of the National Parks Commission), Lord Radnor (Chairman of the Forestry Commission) and Lord Fortescue (the landowner). No record of this meeting survives, and within one month both Lord and Lady Fortescue had died. Local opposition continued. In August 1958 the *North Devon Journal* issued petitions of objection and on 2 October it was able to report that the 'plans may be withdrawn'. On 27 November 1958 the decision was made not to plant conifers on the Chains. Meanwhile, on 29 October 1958 the inaugural meeting of The Exmoor Society was held at Simonsbath Lodge, chaired by John Coleman Cooke. It was not until the 1960s that a Critical Amenity Map was produced for Exmoor in which the Forestry Commission agreed that certain areas should be excluded from planting.

To Plough or not to Plough

In the 1960s a new threat to the character of Exmoor's moorlands emerged: the pressure to increase agricultural productivity coupled with improving farming technology, supported by government grants. This led to plans for agricultural 'improvement' of significant moorland areas.

Geoffrey Sinclair's *'Can Exmoor Survive?'* was published by the Exmoor Society in 1966 and for the first time mapped out and quantified moorland loss. Although the findings were disputed, it seemed to show that moorland was disappearing by 300 hectares (700 acres) a year. The 1960s ploughing grant of £12 an acre was opposed by some members of The Exmoor Society, who feared destruction of flora and fauna as well as accidents with farm machinery on the steep hillsides, but others saw agricultural improvement as essential to preserve Exmoor farms.[196]

During the 1970s the reclamation of moorland for agriculture propelled Exmoor into the national spotlight. In 1976 proposals were put forward to plough up part of the Glenthorne Estate on the A39 near Countisbury. Almost at the same time an area of moorland at Stowey Allotment came up for sale. Following a very low valuation by the County Valuer, the National Park Committee placed an unsuccessful low bid for the land. Within months the new owner gave notice of his intention to plough it up. The fierceness of the debate over moorland loss led to the police being called to the meeting of the National Park Committee on 23 June 1976, with the following headline in the local paper: 'General Steps Out to call Police. Press Gag Foray Shocks National Park Meeting.'[197]

Eventually, in response to an adverse report from the Countryside Commission on the Committee's handling of these issues, the government invited Lord Porchester to carry out an enquiry. The Porchester Enquiry identified the need for proper mapping of land on Exmoor. Production of maps, known as Section 3 Maps, is now a statutory duty of National Park Authorities and identifies land that is of high conservation value. Another outcome of the Porchester Enquiry was the recognition of the need for management agreements. On Exmoor this developed into the first agri-environment scheme in the UK: the Exmoor Farm Conservation Scheme. These agreements compensated landowners for the loss of income that improving their land would have brought them. Eventually this approach evolved into rewarding farmers and landowners for managing their holdings in ways that directly benefited the environment and addressed conservation objectives. From this came the national agri-environment schemes.[198]

IMPRESSIONS OF EXMOOR

Early impressions of the moor do not seem to have inspired outsiders and local people left little in the form of art or literature although Exmoor churches are rich in carving, some possibly inspired by the moor. Early artistic visitors like

Conservation in Action

The National Park designation is intended to conserve and enhance Exmoor's 'natural beauty, wildlife and cultural heritage' and the work of the National Park Authority ranges across the spectrum of conservation.

Damage to Simonsbath sawmill during the major flood event on Exmoor in 1952 (which also led to terrible loss of life and devastation at Lynmouth) saw the end of waterpower at the mill. A large, single cylinder diesel engine was installed and has powered the mill to the present day.

Exmoor National Park Authority bought the sawmill from the Fortescue estate in the 1990s to safeguard the character of the building and its site in the middle of Exmoor, to restore it as a building, and to restore its operation as part of a renewable energy strategy. The mill was purchased with a major grant from the Heritage Lottery Fund. The project consisted of three main elements: reinstatement of the water supply, restoration of the sawmill building itself and overhaul of the sawmilling machinery.

The water supply to the mill, comprising leats, sluices, weir and a water turbine, had not worked since 1952. The leats had to be re-excavated and repaired and the sluice gates serviced. The stone weir, which was built across the river Barle was in reasonable condition but needed some repairs. However, a new fish pass had to be built in order to allow breeding salmon to reach their spawning grounds, which lay upstream of the mill. The restoration of the mill building itself was carried out to the highest building conservation standards.

The restoration of the sawmill was more than a desire to 'preserve' an old structure. It had always been seen as part of the National Park Authority's approach to sustainable countryside management and promotion of the use of renewable energy. To this end, the operating machinery was overhauled. This work involved the repair of the original sawbench, including bringing a working 19th-century sawbench with a 24-inch diameter rotating blade, up to the health and safety requirements of the 21st century. Alongside it stands a new band saw.

Figure A   *Simonsbath sawmill is a 19th-century water-powered mill built for the Knights to serve the Exmoor Forest Estate. It was subsequently used by the Fortescue Estate for processing timber and the production of estate furniture, from floorboards to field gates. It also supplied electricity to parts of Simonsbath village.*

Figure B   *Draft tube repair. The water turbine within the mill building was also in need of major repair, including a replacement draft tube.*

Figure C   *Interior of Simonsbath sawmill in operation. It was opened on 10 June 2003 by HRH The Countess of Wessex. It is a working building once more, used regularly for the processing of timber from Exmoor's woodlands to create gates, fencing and signposts for use around the National Park.*

Figure 110 C. Aldin, *Lady Currie hunting on Exmoor.* Aldin spent his summers at Porlock travelling over the surrounding moors and sold his paintings, as did Edwards, at Porlock parish rooms.

Thomas Rowlandson, J.M. Turner and Devon clergyman, John Swete, were more interested in the coast, buildings and estates than the moorland. By the 19th century tastes were changing towards an appreciation of wild, romantic landscapes. Views of Exmoor were produced as book illustrations or in the early 20th century as covers for tourist maps. John William North

Figure 111 A. Munnings, *Barle at Brightworthy,* Withypool, 1942. His painting of Mill Hill, Oare captures the smooth brown of the moors in autumn with sharp clarity whereas this wartime summer view of the Barle is more impressionistic.

(1842-1924) painted at Exford but Frederick Walker, George Pinwell, Hubert von Herkomer, and Robert McBeth preferred the Quantocks and the coast, finding the rain and mists of Exmoor uncongenial to painting.

Artists

It was the sporting artists including Cecil Aldin (1870-1935), Robert Polhill Bevan (1865-1925), Lionel Edwards (1878-1966), and Sir Alfred Munnings (1878-1959) who were inspired to paint the moors. Bevan took up residence at Hawkridge in the 1890s and Alfred Munnings, formerly part of the Newlyn School, visited Exmoor to hunt. Many local people remember him and his wife, Violet, because they came to live at Withypool between 1940 and 1945, their house in Essex having been requisitioned. He painted landscapes, sheep, ponies and occasionally local people. He was also a sculptor and wrote ballad poems including *Larkbarrow Farm* in 1938.

Other artists of Exmoor include Lucy Kemp Welch (1869-1958), one of the first to capture the swiftness of Exmoor's deer and ponies on the move, and Alexander Carruthers Gould (1870-1948) whose work as a lumberman in the First World War may explain his exuberant portrayal of trees, seen marching up the valley accompanied by red deer and birds in flight in his painting of Dunkery. Since the mid-20th century books and materials designed to draw people to Exmoor have used photographers rather than artists. Fine photographers like Alfred Vowles, James Ravilious, and Jasper Bowden have portrayed Exmoor.[199]

Figure 112 Ann le Bas RA (b.1923). Artists are still drawn to southern Exmoor, notably Winsford, including Ann le Bas, Hilary Adair and 'Sandy' Lines (1922-2002) who produced watercolours of Exmoor. People still come to Exmoor in search of artistic inspiration.

Figure 113 R.D. Blackmore, author of *Lorna Doone*, which has spawned over a century of tourism since it was published. By 1895 Exmoor was described as *Lorna Doone* country and from the 1930s books sought to turn the novel into historical fact and guide tourists to specific locations.

Writers

Exmoor has inspired many writers but few books have promoted Exmoor or had such an impact on the area as Richard Dodderidge Blackmore's *Lorna Doone* (1869). Visitors flock to 'Doone valley' and Lorna Doone Farm. Even the Ordnance Survey locates 'Doone Country' on its Explorer map of Exmoor. Richard Jefferies wrote *Red Deer* (1884) after a visit to Exmoor with his friend, the painter John William North. He ate clotted cream and jam at Tarr Steps and noted on his return the labourers going home through Dulverton with tree branches for the family hearth across their shoulders. He observed Exmoor life including whortleberry picking, still a popular custom although no longer producing 'tons and tons – whole truck loads – sent away by railroad'. Even more popular was Sir John Fortescue's *The Story of a Red Deer* (1897) written for children.

Hope Bourne lived for many years at Higher Blackland Farm, Withypool and in a caravan at Ferny Ball, Exmoor. She lived a frugal life, shooting rabbits and pigeons for food and taught herself to write and paint. Her articles and books such as *Living on Exmoor* (1963) and *Wild Harvest* (1978) have attracted visitors. Late 20th-century social historian Berta Lawrence was a poet who wrote *Deserted Village* about Clicket, near Timberscombe. The opening words of the poem could apply to any of Exmoor's abandoned settlements. 'Dead now, old people who remembered'.[200]

Figure 114 Exford from a drawing by John William North. He illustrated the works of his friend the writer and mystic Richard Jefferies (1848-87) but failed to establish an Exmoor school of painters.

TOURISM

People have been drawn to Exmoor's wild beauty for two hundred years or more and by the 20th century tourists were no longer exclusively from the leisured class, nor only there for the sport. Artists and writers, especially R.D. Blackmore, were influenced by Exmoor and drew others to see it for themselves.

In summer and during the hunting season visitors occupied all the available accommodation, and their grooms and chauffeurs lodged in village houses. A Simonsbath cottage provided teas, and one farmhouse and the vicarage were let as hunting boxes in the autumn, which augmented incomes. By necessity, hosts had to be creative and enterprising, so farmers provided stables for visitors' horses and some bought ponies to hire out. *The White Horse* at Exford, which in 1910 had 13 bedrooms and two bathrooms, had a livery stable and accommodation for cars, while the *Exmoor Forest Hotel* offered 12 bedrooms, two bathrooms, electric lighting, ample stabling, and a cycle house, and fetched visitors from Dulverton station in the 1920s. The hotel was open all year as people came for hunting, bringing their own horses often for a month or more. After a large breakfast most guests collected a packed lunch leaving the hotel free for coach parties from Minehead and Lynmouth and others wanting lunches and cream teas.

By the time the Second World War broke out there were private hotels and boarding houses in most villages. There

Figure 115 Tarr Steps c.1890 with William Bidgood, engraver of the Steps and other views. Cheap rail excursions, charabancs and coaches brought day trippers to places like Tarr Steps. Holidaymakers on the coast visited the moors on organised outings from their hotel or resort.

were hunting stables at Winsford and Exford, which also had a youth hostel, and in 1939 the *Lion Hotel* at Dulverton advertised itself as a sportsman's hotel offering economical hacking and hunting. The war had an adverse effect on the tourist trade but there was an influx of soldiers, evacuees, and refugees from the south-east. As a result, one couple who converted a Winsford shop into a guesthouse and teashop at the beginning of the war soon found themselves with semi-permanent guests. The Exmoor souvenir trade, which now extends from books and postcards to hand-crafted items also began in earnest at this time, when an enterprising shopkeeper in Dulverton sent a photograph of the bridge and cottages to Ireland to be made into linen tea towels.[201]

After the war holidaymakers returned and by the 1950s, as austerity gave way to the means for enjoyment, a week or a fortnight by the sea came within the reach of greater numbers. By 1952 Dulverton station was a point of arrival for thousands of Exmoor visitors. The railway enabled people from all over the country to visit Exmoor easily. Camping and caravanning were popular and young people explored the countryside by bicycle or on foot. In 1962 Butlin's Holiday Camp opened at Minehead drawing thousands to West Somerset and Exmoor. Village shops were stocked with ice cream and picture postcards and it seemed everyone provided cream teas.

In the late 20th and early 21st centuries some traditional hotels like the *Carnarvon Arms* have closed, but self-catering accommodation has become more popular. This can include anything from the caravan and camping parks at Dulverton, Exford and Winsford to the labourers' cottages and barns that have been converted into holiday homes at Wintershead, Riscombe and Lambscombe. There are also lodges in East Anstey and bed and breakfasts run by many farms and village houses. By the early 21st century Exford had six hotels and guesthouses offering around seventy rooms, and several village houses were available to let. Even the smaller villages usually have a tearoom or a restaurant. The Simonsbath House site comprises hotel, restaurant and holiday apartments.

Pony trekkers and cyclists come to enjoy the moors, as do walkers, who make the most of the long distance footpaths such as the Macmillan and Samaritans ways. Land Rover safaris and walkers' buses reduce car use, and several properties still take visitors' horses or offer riding. Exford youth hostel offers courses and activity holidays and sailing and other watersports are provided on Wimbleball Lake, a large reservoir two miles west of Dulverton.

THE FUTURE FOR SOUTHERN EXMOOR?

The foot and mouth outbreak of 2001, which restricted access
to Exmoor, finally proved that, as in other upland areas, the
local economy is dependent on recreation and tourism, rather
than agriculture. Losses of 50 to 100 per cent of income were
reported by local businesses, including shops, which depended on
visitors but farming remains essential to providing the managed
landscape with animals that tourists come to see and the local
produce they increasingly expect to buy while on holiday. There
are inevitable conflicts between modern 'industrial' farming and
the historic landscape, but government policy and moves towards
sustainable farming may reduce that in years to come. The 'right
to roam' brings increasing pressure on land owners to enable
recreational use. The natural beauty of the landscape and its
wildlife and the wealth of archaeological remains, which survive
so well in upland habitats, are probably more at risk from visitors
than farmers. The many sporting activities such as cycling,
designed to encourage out of season tourism, could damage the
area if not carefully managed.

It seems unlikely that the settlement pattern of Exmoor will
change greatly in the foreseeable future. Planning restrictions
constrain new development but Dulverton and Brushford have
new houses and villages such as East Anstey, which are seeing their
populations rise again, will be expanded on a small scale to meet
housing needs. Meanwhile, Exmoor's popularity with those who
can afford second homes and the rise in self-catering holidays,
even at the upper end of the market, will probably prevent

Figure 116 Exford,
a village dependent
on tourism. Exmoor's
settlements can no longer
'go it alone' but depend on
resources from incomers,
commuters, visitors and
others to survive.

more houses being abandoned. As both a National Park and an Environmentally Sensitive Area, it seems unlikely that Exmoor will ever again see settlement schemes like those of the Knights, but southern Exmoor's villages and farms will change as people adapt to alterations in the population, economy and climate in order to survive in their English upland.

Endnotes

CHAPTER 1 Southern Exmoor, pp. 1-9

1   Bates, E.H., 'Leland in Somersetshire', *Somerset Archaeological and Natural History Society (SANHS) Proceedings* (1888), 40; Bonham-Carter, V., *Exmoor Writers and their Works* (Dulverton, 1987); Pollard, S., *Marginal Europe: the Contribution of Marginal lands since the Middle Ages* (Oxford, 1997), 12-20, 32, 54-88, 122-31, 164, 199, 240; Winchester, A.J.L., *The Harvest of the Hills: Rural Life in Northern England and the Scottish Borders 1400-1700* (Edinburgh, 2008), 3-150.

2   Bates, E.H., 'Leland in Somersetshire', *SANHS Proceedings* (1888), 40.

3   Cornwell, J., *Earth to Earth* (1982), 39. Comment on a family of farmers who killed themselves in 1975 rather than leave their Devon farm.

4   Somerset RO, Exmoor Oral Archive.

CHAPTER 2 The Earliest Settlement, pp. 11-27

5   Malone, C., *Neolithic Britain and Ireland* (2006), 30.

6   Albrethsen, S.E. and Petersen, B.E., 'Excavation of a Mesolithic Cemetery at Vedbæk, Denmark' *Acta Archaeologica*, 47 (1976), 1-28; Conneller, C. and Warren, G. (eds.), *Mesolithic Britain and Ireland, New Approaches* (2006), 161.

7   (Gradual transition to farming) Malone, C., *Neolithic Britain and Ireland* (2006), 22; (Mes./Neolithic woodland decline); Rippon, S., 'Landscapes of Pre-Medieval Occupation' in Kain, R. (ed.), *England's Landscape – The South West* (English Heritage, 2006), 46.

8   Malone, C., *Neolithic Britain and Ireland* (2006), 165, 188; Riley, H. and Wilson-North, R., *The Field Archaeology of Exmoor* (English Heritage, 2001), 24; Burl, A., *The Stone Circles of Britain, Ireland and Brittany* (Yale, 2000).

9   Malone, C., *Neolithic Britain and Ireland* (2006), 187; Burl, A., *From Carnace to Callanish – the Prehistoric Stone Rows and Avenues of Britain, Ireland and Brittany* (Yale, 1993), 88.

10   Information from Mark Gillings, April 2007.

11   Information from T. Green.

12   Woodward, A., *British Barrows – A Matter of Life and Death* (2002), 50.

13   Riley, H. and Wilson-North, R., *The Field Archaeology of Exmoor* (English Heritage, 2001), 37; Woodward, A., *British Barrows – A Matter of Life and Death* (2002), 128; Juleff, G. and Bray, L., forthcoming.

14   Excavation by H. Quinnell; Woodward, A., *British Barrows – A Matter of Life and Death* (2002), 49-50.

15   Riley, H. and Wilson-North, R., *The Field Archaeology of Exmoor* (English Heritage, 2001), 65.

16   Cunliffe, B., *Iron Age Communities in Britain* (1991), 537.

17   Thomas, C., 'The character and origins of Roman Dumnonia', *Rural Settlement in Roman Britain* (CBA, 1966), 74-8.

18   Webster, C. and Mayberry, T. (eds.), *The Archaeology of Somerset* (2007), 47, 49-50.

19   Information from Gill Juleff and Lee Bray.

CHAPTER 3 The Anglo-Saxon Centuries, pp. 29-47

20   See chapter 2; Thorn, C. and F., *Domesday Book: Devon* (Chichester, 1985);
     Domesday Book: Somerset (Chichester, 1980), have indexes of all places
     mentioned and translations of all entries.

21   Webster, C. and Mayberry, T. (eds.), *The Archaeology of Somerset* (Taunton, 2007), 60.

22   Welch, M., 'Migrating Hordes', *The Land of the Dobunni* (2003), 65-6.

23   Fyfe, R., Rippon, S. and Brown, T., 'Pollen, farming and history in
     Greater Exmoor', *Current Archaeology* (192, 2004), 564-7; Fyfe, R.,
     'Palaeoenvironmental perspectives on medieval landscape development',
     Turner, S. (ed.), *Medieval Devon and Cornwall: Shaping an Ancient Countryside*
     (Macclesfield, 2006), p.18.

24   Riley, H. and Wilson-North, R., *The Field Archaeology of Exmoor* (English
     Heritage, 2001), 100; Fox, H., 'Foreword' in Turner, S., *Medieval Devon and
     Cornwall*, pp.ix-xvi.

25   Rippon, S., Fyfe, R. and Brown, A.G., 'Beyond Villages and Open Fields: The
     Origins and Development of a Historic Landscape Characterised by Dispersed
     Settlement in South-West England', *Medieval Archaeology* (50, 2006), 49.

26   Yorke, B., *Wessex in the Early Middle Ages* (1995), 87.

27   *Ibid.* 85-6.

28   MacDermot, E.T., *A History of the Forest of Exmoor* (1973), 15; see chapter 4.

29   Winchester, A.J.L., 'Moorland forests of medieval England', in Whyte, I.D. and
     Winchester, A.J.L. (eds.), *Society, Landscape and Environment in Upland Britain*
     (Birmingham, 2004), 34.

30   See chapter 4.

31   M. Aston, 'Early Monasteries in Somerset', *The Land of the Dobunni*, 38-9.

32   Riley, H. and Wilson-North, R., *The Field Archaeology of Exmoor* (English
     Heritage, 2001), 88-9.

33   Blair, J., *The Church in Anglo-Saxon Society* (Oxford, 2005), 302-5, 426; Turner,
     S., *Making a Christian Landscape* (Exeter, 2006), 51, 135, 152-4.

34   Farmer, D.H., *The Oxford Dictionary of Saints* (Oxford, 1992), 395-6; Blair, J.,
     The Church in Anglo-Saxon Society (Oxford, 2005), 244-5.

35   TNA, SP 15/14/91; see R. Faith, 'Cola's *tun*: rural social structure in late Anglo-
     Saxon Devon', in Evans, R. (ed.), *Lordship and Learning: Studies in Memory of
     Trevor Aston* (Woodbridge, 2004), 63-78, for a detailed analysis of Anglo-Saxon
     social structure in the South Hams of Devon.

36   Lennard, R., *Rural England 1086-1135* (Oxford, 1959), p.342; Faith, R., *The
     English Peasantry and the Growth of Lordship* (1997), pp.70-4; Dyer, C., *Making
     a living in the Middle Ages: the people of Britain, 850-1520* (2003), 38.

37   Leahy, K., *Anglo-Saxon Crafts* (Stroud, 2003), 168-9; Dyer, C., *Making a living
     in the Middle Ages: the people of Britain, 850-1520* (2003), 36.

38   When granted to William de Wrotham in 1198, the estate of Robert of
     Auberville included Hawkridge and Withypool: charter cited in MacDermot,
     E.T., *A History of the Forest of Exmoor* (1973), 107. William and other Royal
     Foresters held Newton Forester, North Petherton: *VCH Somerset*, VI, 285-6.

39   Keats-Rohan, K., *Domesday People: a prosopography of persons occurring in
     English documents 1066-1166* (Woodbridge, 1999).

40   For an analysis of Domesday statistics and terms see Darby, H.C., *The
     Domesday Geography of South-West England* (Cambridge, 1967); for a study
     of one manor, Pinbury in Gloucestershire, with the help of a survey that was
     taken only 34 years later see Dyer, C., *Making a living in the Middle Ages: the
     people of Britain, 850-1520* (2003), 90-4.

41   Darby, H.C., *Domesday England* (Cambridge, 1977), 90-3.

42   Riley, H. and Wilson-North, R., *The Field Archaeology of Exmoor* (English
     Heritage, 2001), 100; Fox, H., 'Foreword' in Turner, S., *Medieval Devon and
     Cornwall*, pp.ix-xvi; see chapter 4.

CHAPTER 4 The Middle Ages, pp. 49-67

43 MacDermot, E.T., *A History of the Forest of Exmoor* (1911; new edn, Newton Abbot, 1973), 66-73; *VCH Somerset*, VI, 285-8; Hobbs, S. (ed.), *The Cartulary of Forde Abbey* (Somerset Record Society 85, 1998), p.123.

44 MacDermot, E.T., *A History of the Forest of Exmoor* (1973), 79-91.

45 *Ibid.* 55.

46 *Ibid.* 46-7, 91, 101, 137-59.

47 Chadwyck-Healey, C.E.H., *Somersetshire Pleas c.1200-1256*, p.107; Glasscock, R.E., *The Subsidy of 1334*, 265; (Royal income from forest and branding of animals) MacDermot, E.T., *A History of the Forest of Exmoor* (1973), 181-218, 451-2; SRO, tithe awards, Hawkridge and Withypool.

48 Cowley, F.G., *The Monastic Order in S. Wales, 1066-1349*, p.76, citing *Statuta Capitulorum Generalium Ordinis Cisterciensis*, J.M. Canivez (ed.) (1933-9), I, pp.235-6; SRO, A/AHT 3, 4; *ibid.* DD/L P 16/4, 7-8.

49 Dickinson, F.H. (ed.), *Kirby's Quest for Somerset* (Somerset Record Society, 3, 1889), 178-81; TNA, C 135/1/2; BL, Add. Ch. 7671.

50 Chadwyck-Healey, C.E.H., *Somersetshire Pleas c.1200-1256*, p.302.

51 Summerson, H. (ed.), *Crown Pleas of the Devon Eyre of 1238* (Devon and Cornwall Record Society, NS 28, Torquay, 1985), 52, 55; MacDermot, E.T., *A History of the Forest of Exmoor* (1973), 79-91; Rippon, S., Fyfe, R. and Brown, A.G., 'Beyond Villages and Open Fields: The Origins and Development of a Historic Landscape Characterised by Dispersed Settlement in South-West England', *Medieval Archaeology*, 50 (2006), 62.

52 *VCH Devon*, I, foreword.

53 SRO, DD/SAS PD 148; Gover, J.E.B., Mawer, A. and Stenton, F.M. (eds.), *Place Names of Devon* (Cambridge, 1931-2), II. 335, 337, 343-4, 354; Chadwyck-Healey, C.E.H., *Somersetshire Pleas c.1200-1256*, 302, 322; MacDermot, E.T., *A History of the Forest of Exmoor* (1973), 84-91.

54 TNA, C133/4/7; Dickinson, F.H. (ed.), *Kirby's Quest for Somerset* (Somerset Record Society, 3, 1889), 178-81; OS Map 1:25,000 OL9 (2005 edn).

55 MacDermot, E.T., *A History of the Forest of Exmoor* (1973), 81, 99 Hobbs, S. (ed.), *The Cartulary of Forde Abbey* (Somerset Record Society 85, 1998), p.123; Somerset CC, HER; SRO, DD/SF 2/78/2.

56 Rippon, S., Fyfe, R. and Brown, A.G., 'Beyond Villages and Open Fields', *Medieval Archaeology* (2006), 64-7; SRO, Exford tithe award.

57 SRO, A/BCQ 1.

58 Hobbs, S. (ed.), *The Cartulary of Forde Abbey* (Somerset Record Society 85, 1998), p.176; MacDermot, E.T., *A History of the Forest of Exmoor* (1973), 90, 96, 99; SRO, DD/SF 2/78/2.

59 Chadwyck-Healey, C.E.H., *Somersetshire Pleas c.1200-1256*, pp.388-9, 391-4, 404-5; Winchester, A.J.L., *The Harvest of the Hills*, passim.

60 Dickinson, F.H. (ed.), *Kirby's Quest for Somerset* (Somerset Record Society, 3, 1889), 178-81, 248: only those who can be definitely assigned to parishes have been included in the figures; *Cal. Fine R. 1307-19*, 126, 141, 144; *Cal. Close, 1313-18*, 52; *Cal. Chart. R. 1300-26*, 68; SRO, A/AHT 3.

61 TNA, C134/33/6 and manor extents printed in Annett, *North Molton*, p.61; Holmes, T.S. (ed.), *Register of Bishop Ralph of Shrewsbury* (Somerset Record Society 10, 1896).

62 Fenwick, C.C. (ed.), *The Poll Taxes of 1377, 1379, and 1381* (Oxford, 1998); TNA E 179/169/150; DRO, 248M/M4; Dickinson, F.H. (ed.), *Kirby's Quest for Somerset* (Somerset Record Society, 3, 1889), 178-81; TNA, E 179/97/194 (1525) printed in Stoate, T.L. (ed.), *Devon Subsidy Rolls 1524-7* (Bristol, 1979); Somerset CC, HER.

63 SRO, A/AHT 4.

CHAPTER 5 Reformation to Interregnum, 1560-1654, pp. 69-85

64 MacDermot, E.T., *A History of the Forest of Exmoor* (1973), 248.
65 (Quote from Sir John Poyntz) *Ibid.* 229.
66 (Loss of sheep) *Ibid.* 272.
67 *Ibid.* 302.
68 *Ibid.* (see n.143), 220-9, 237-41, 245-52, 276, 287-94, 299, 316-20.
69 (Travellers buried at Brushford) SRO, D/P/brush 2/1/1; D/P/dul 2/1/1.
70 Webb, A.J., *Two Tudor Subsidy Assessments* (Somerset Record Society 88, 2002), 110, 112-13, 188; Stoate, T.L. (ed.), *Devon Taxes 1581-1660* (Bristol, *c.*1988), 24-5.
71 *Valor Ecclesiasticus, temp. Hen. VIII* (Record Commission, 1810), I, 223, II, 346.
72 SRO, DD/SF 1/3/5; D/D/Ct H102A; DD/SP inventories; *ibid.* Q/SR 11/88, 15/22, 81/129.
73 TNA, C 1/466/55; *ibid.* E 179/169/50; Weaver, F.W. (ed.), *Wells Wills* (1890), 73; Hare, J., 'Pensford and the growth of the cloth industry in late medieval Somerset', *Proc. Som. Arch. Soc.* (147, 2004), 173-80.
74 TNA, C 1/886/25; C 1/1421/8-9.
75 ('great ruin and decay') *Cal Pat.* 1555-7, pp.18-19; (disposal of market revenues) TNA, REQ 2, 30/3, 31/64, 77/77, 113/36.
76 SRO, Q/SR 32/92; (Wills) *ibid.* D/D/Ct T55; DD/SF 1/3/43; *ibid.* A/AHT 1/7; Siraut, M. (ed.), *Somerset Wills* (Somerset Record Society 89, 2003), 35.
77 SRO, DD/SF 1/2/24, 1/3/5.
78 Weaver, F.W. (ed.), *Wells Wills* (1890), 73-5, 82-5, 196-200; SRO, D/D/Ct N 87; DD/SF 1/2/24.
79 Weaver, F.W. (ed.), *Wells Wills* (1890), 73-5, 82-5, 196-200; SRO, A/AZW 1.
80 For Morebath see Duffy, E., *The Voices of Morebath* (Yale, 2001); Rose-Troup, F., *The Western Rebellion of 1549* (1913), 319 (gives Oxford in error), 498.
81 Green, E. (ed.), *Certificate of Musters, 1569* (Somerset Record Society 20, 1904) 48, 158-9, 163-4; SRO, D/P/wins 4/1/3.
82 SRO, Q/SR 2/67, 38/82; *ibid.* DD/WO 55/7/12.
83 *Cal Pat.* 1555-7, pp.18-19.
84 SRO, DD/SP inventories 1636; *ibid.* Q/SR 3/22.
85 Underdown, D., *Revel, Riot, and Rebellion* (Oxford, 1987), 178.
86 Chadwyck Healey, C.E.H. (ed.), *Bellum Civile: Hopton's Narrative of his Campaign in the West, 1642-4* (Somerset Record Society 18, 1902), 18-19; *Cal. Cttee. for Compounding*, I, 1610; II, 1234.
87 Devon RO, QS/128/85/1, 3.
88 SRO, D/P/wins 4/1/3, 13/2/1.

CHAPTER 6 After the Civil War, 1654-1815, pp. 87-105

89 Stevens, D., *War and Peace in West Somerset 1620-1670* (Minehead, 1988), 77-8, 82.
90 Dick, O.L. (ed.), *Aubrey's Brief Lives* (1972 edn), 192-5; *DNB*.
91 MacDermot, E.T., *A History of the Forest of Exmoor* (1973), 211-12, 394; SRO, Q/SR 298/81; 1782 map reprinted in Harley, J.B. and Dunning, R.W. (eds.), *Somerset Maps* (Somerset Record Society 76, 1981); MacDermot, E.T., *A History of the Forest of Exmoor* (1973), 330, 337-42, 379-80, 383; Devon RO 1148M add 11/8; SRO, DD/X/ETH 1.
92 SRO, Q/RLa 22/15, 17; DD/X/ETH 1; DD/SP inventory 1694/9.
93 SRO, DD/TB 23/28/11; DD/SP 1669/69; *ibid.* A/AHT 28, 54, 113,115; Siraut, M. (ed.), *Somerset Wills* (Somerset Record Society 89, 2003), 231.
94 *Home Office Acreage Returns (HO 67)* II (List and Index Society 189-90, 1982). No returns for East and West Anstey, Exmoor, Hawkridge or Withypool; SRO, DD/cwc.ta 21; DD/SP 1730/7; DD/SY 3; Devon RO 1148M/add 6/14.
95 SRO, DD/TRANS 3/7; Defoe, D., *A Tour Through the Whole Island of Great Britain, Letter 4, Part 1: North Cornwall and Devon*; Winchester, A.J.L., *Harvest of the Hills*, 79-82, 96.

96   Highclere Castle, V/A8; SRO, DD/SP 1741/11.

97   Wade Martins, S., *The English Model Farm: Building the Agricultural Ideal, 1700-1914* (Macclesfield, 2002), 78; *Farmers, Landlords and Landscapes* (Macclesfield, 2004), 113; Riley, H. and Wilson-North, R., *The Field Archaeology of Exmoor* (English Heritage, 2001), 128-9; Somerset CC, HER.

98   SRO, A/AQP 8, 37; *Exeter Flying Post*, 31 July 1794.

99   Billingsley, J., *General View of Agriculture of Somerset* (Bath, 1798), 173-5.

100 Vancouver, C., *General View of the agriculture of the County of Devon with observations on the means of its improvement* (1808), 100-1, 338; for breeding, see next chapter.

101 SRO, A/CRZ 2/3; *ibid.* DD/X/HDG 2-6.

102 Bates, E.H. (ed.), *Gerard's Survey of Somerset, 1633* (Somerset Record Society 15, 1900), 7; SRO, Q/SR 41/58, 111/63, 112/66, 193/9.

103 SRO, A/AQP 37.

104 (Households with servants) SRO, D/P/dul 2/1/1; DD/WY 34; Howard, A.J. and Stoate, T.L. (eds.), *Somerset Protestation Returns* (Bristol, 1975), 157-8.

105 SRO, DD/SF 1/3/43, 2/67/38; DD/SP 1680/84; *ibid.* A/AHT 75, 129; *ibid.* Q/SR 111/16; Shakespeare Birthplace Trust RO DR 5/573, cat. on A2A website; SRO, A/AQP 37; *ibid.* DD/SF 3112; Census (1801, 1811); Swete, J., *Travels in Georgian Devon*, T. Gray (ed.), III (Tiverton, 1999), 57; TNA, HO 107/965.

106 SRO, DD/X/CH 1; DD/SP 1682/54; 1683/98; 1684/73, 1721/12; *ibid.* Q/SR 207/2; TNA, PROB 11/1284.

107 SRO, A/AHT 40, 42; *ibid.* DD/X/DL 1/1-3; Binding, H. and Bonham-Carter, V., *Old Dulverton*, 12.

108 Siraut, *Somerset Wills*, 57; SRO, DD/SF 2/9/5; Highclere Castle, V/A8; Census (1801).

109 Riley, H. and Wilson-North, R., *The Field Archaeology of Exmoor* (English Heritage, 2001), 111-12; SRO, A/AQP 8; *ibid.* DD/DP 9/14; Hoskins, W.G., *Devon* (1954), 138, 140.

110 SRO, DD/SF 5/6/29; 10/3/26; 12/15/28.

111 Shakespeare Birthplace Trust RO, DR 5/562, cat. on A2A website.

112 Highclere Castle, V/A3, 5; SRO, Q/REl 22/15, 41/10; *ibid.* A/AHT 174/3; *Western Flying Post*, 25 May 1795.

113 Morland, S.C. (ed.), *The Somersetshire Quarterly Meeting of the Society of Friends 1668-1699* (Somerset Record Society 75, 1978), 60-1, 69, 71, 73; Turner, G.L. (ed.), *Original Records of Early Nonconformity under Persecution and Indulgence* (1911-14), II, 111; Gordon, A., *Freedom after Ejection* (Manchester, 1917), 93-5; SRO, DD/BR/py 57; *Annual Report of the Somerset Congregational Union* (1896); *DNB*.

114 Hoskins, *Devon*, 240; Symons, W., *Early Methodism in West Somerset and the Lorna Doone country* (1895), 81.

115 SRO, A/AQP 37.

116 *Exeter Flying Post* 19 Sep 1805; Highclere Castle, KK/A1; SRO, D/D/Vc 88, *ibid.* A/AQP 8; *Digest of Returns to the Select Committee on the Education of the Poor* (Parl. Papers 1819) (224) ix (2).

117 SRO, D/P/wins 13/3/17-18; Census.

118 SRO, A/AQP 8.

CHAPTER 7 The Exmoor Experiment, 1815-1910, pp. 107-23

119 *Ibid.* A/BAZ 1/3; *ibid.* Q/RDe 140.

120 *Ibid*, Q/RDe 140; OS Map 1:10560, Som. XLV. NW; OS Map 1:2500, Som. XLV.5 (1903 edn).

121 Harley, J.B. and Dunning, R.W. (ed.), *Somerset Maps* (Somerset Record Society 76, 1981), map, 1822; OS Map 1:2500, Som. XLV.5 (1903 edn); C. Garrett, 'An Enviable Possession', *Exmoor Review* (2005), 75-7.

122 Census; Orwin, C.S. and Sellick, R.J., *The Reclamation of Exmoor Forest* (Newton Abbot, 1970), 61.

123 Orwin, C.S. and Sellick, R.J., *The Reclamation of Exmoor Forest* (Newton Abbot, 1970), 64-6; SRO, A/BAZ 1/3.

124 TNA, HO 107/965/14; Orwin, C.S. and Sellick, R.J., *The Reclamation of Exmoor Forest* (Newton Abbot, 1970), 115.

125 Orwin, C.S. and Sellick, R.J., *The Reclamation of Exmoor Forest* (Newton Abbot, 1970), 255.

126 *Ibid.* (see n.143), 241-56.

127 TNA, IR 18/1186, 8551; Hoskins, W., *Devon*, 91; Acland, T.D. and Sturge, W., *The Farming of Somersetshire* (1851), 20-1; inf. from website of Devon Cattle Breeders' Society of Australia; TNA, HO 107/235.

128 SCC, HER; *ibid.* IR 18/1186, 1405, 1546, 8551, 8868.

129 TNA, IR 1186-7, 1405, 1546, 8444, 8551, 8567, 8594, 8853, 8868. There is no survey of Exmoor district and no livestock returns for the Ansteys or Molland and no acreages for West Anstey. Devon RO, tithe awards East and West Anstey, Molland, Twitchen; SRO, tithe awards Brushford, Dulverton, Exford, Hawkridge, Winsford, Withypool.

130 SRO, DD/X/MT 3; Acland, T.D. and Sturge, W., *The Farming of Somersetshire* (1851), 10-1; Devon RO, B4159/10; N. Devon RO, B445/13; Som. CC, HER.

131 Census (1811-41); TNA, HO 107/235, 965; SRO, D/P/dul 2/1/7, 4/1/1-2; D/P/brush 2/1/3.

132 M. Lyte, 'Regional Agricultural Wage Variation in early 19th-century England', *Agricultural History Review* (55, 2007), 95-9; *Abridgement of the Abstract of the Answers and Returns … so far as relates to the poor* (HC 1818), 382-3, 394-5.

133 SRO, D/P/wins 13/2/5; Census (1821); TNA, HO 107/235, 965.

134 SRO, D/P/wins 13/3/17-23.

135 *Ibid*, D/G/d 134/1, 136/10.

136 *Ibid.* D/P/dul 2/1/6, 4/1/1; *ibid.* D/G/d 134/1, 136/10; TNA, IR 18/8551; *ibid.* HO 107/965.

137 North Devon RO B49/add 2/1; TNA, RG 11/2241.

CHAPTER 8 The Rise and Fall of High Farming, 1845-1910, pp. 125-47

138 Acland, T.D. and Sturge, W., *The Farming of Somersetshire* (1851), 28-31; TNA, HO 107/1890.

139 Acland, T.D. and Sturge, W., *The Farming of Somersetshire* (1851), 28-31; see previous chapter. Hannam's diary is in the Bodleian Library, Oxford.

140 TNA, HO 107/1890; *ibid*. RG 13/2266; MacDermot, E.T., *A History of the Forest of Exmoor* (1973), 440; Orwin, C.S. and Sellick, R.J., *The Reclamation of Exmoor Forest* (Newton Abbot, 1970), 222-231.

141 TNA, MAF 68/60, 486, 1056; Orwin, C.S. and Sellick, R.J., *The Reclamation of Exmoor Forest* (Newton Abbot, 1970), 124-7.

142 Orwin, C.S. and Sellick, R.J., *The Reclamation of Exmoor Forest* (Newton Abbot, 1970), 116-17.

143 *Ibid.* 132-5.

144 TNA, MAF 68/60, 486, 1056, 1626, 2196; *First Report on Agricultural Depression: Report by Assistant Commissioner on North Devon* (C-7728) HC (1894) xvi, 6-10, 15, 50-1.

145 IR 58/4605, 4778, 4980, 82357, 82400.

146 *Ibid.* IR 58/82400.

147 SRO, Q/RDe 60a, 80a, 146, 150; TNA, MAF 1/131; Acland, T.D. and Sturge, W., *The Farming of Somersetshire* (1851), 27.

148 TNA, MAF 68/1056, 1626.

149 TNA, HO 107/1891; *ibid*. IR 58/4778; OS Map 1:10560 Som. LXV.SE (1906 edn).

150 TNA, HO 107/1890-1.

151   *Ibid.* MAF 68/60; *Report of the Royal Commission on Children, Young Persons, and Women in Agriculture* (Parl. Papers 1868-9 (4202), xiii, 451-5.

152   TNA RG 11/2239, 2242, 2358.

153   *Ibid.* MAF 68/1626, 2196; statistics supplied by the then Bd. of Agric., 1905; inf. from Exmoor Horn Society's website.

154   M. Deering, 'A hamlet in history', *Exmoor Review* (1990), 46-9; *Report on Children, Young Persons, and Women in Agriculture*, 451-5; TNA, HO 107/1891.

155   *Report on Children, Young Persons, and Women in Agriculture*, 451-5; *First Report on Agricultural Depression: North Devon*, 6-10, 15, 26, 50-1.

156   D.W. Warren, 'Newland Quarry', *Journal of Somerset Industrial Archaeological Society*, 2, 36-9; TNA, RG 11/2358.

157   Orwin, C.S. and Sellick, R.J., *The Reclamation of Exmoor Forest* (Newton Abbot, 1970), 172-78; J. Hurley, *Murder and Mystery on Exmoor* (1972 edn), 16-19.

158   Burt, R., Waite, P. and Burnley R., *Devon and Somerset Mines* (Exeter, 1984), 5-6, 19-20, 53, 80, 84-5, 126-7; TNA, HO 107/1891; *ibid.* RG 11/2239; RG 12/1769; RG 13/2140, 2266.

159   TNA, BT 31/436/1682; BT 31/2061/9080; *ibid.* RG 10/2180; RG 11/2358; Devon RO 96M/box 94/8; SRO, A/BAZ 4.16.11.10, 43; *Journal of Bath and West of England Society*, VI (1858), 345.

160   TNA, RG 10/2358; RG 11/2358; SRO, D/P/winsf 2/1/10; Som. CC, HER; Sellick, R., *The West Somerset Mineral Railway* (1970), 74; M.H. Jones, 'Wartime Mining on Exmoor', *Exmoor Review* (1979), 41-2.

161   Acland, T.D. and Sturge, W., *The Farming of Somersetshire* (1851), 25; TNA, HO 107/1890-1; SRO, D/P/wins 2/1/11; *Report on Children, Young Persons, and Women in Agriculture*, 451-5.

162   SRO, D/G/d 139/1.

163   TNA, RG 9/1606; RG 11/2358, RG 13/2266; (Jane Morley) SRO, D/G/d 38/1, 60/1; North Devon RO, Molland vestry books; (South Molton workhouse) www.workhouses.org.uk (S. Molton).

164   SRO, D/G/d 67/1, 69/1. Exmoor parish was not in Dulverton union in the 19th century.

165   Census (1901); TNA, RG 13/2139-40, 2266.

166   SRO, D/P/wins 2/1/11; TNA, RG11/2358; *DNB*.

167   *Report on Children, Young Persons, and Women in Agriculture*, 451-5; SRO, C/E 4/380.

168   *Kelly's Dir. Devon* (1875); *Kelly's Dir. Som.* (1906); SRO, D/N/wsc 3/2/3.

169   Pevsner, N., *South and West Somerset* (1958), 152, 348, 350; North Devon RO, Molland parish records.

170   Wilts RO 2515/406/1408; SRO, Q/RUP/380; *ibid.* A/BAZ 4/11; MacDermot, E.T., *History of the Great Western Railway*, rev. C R Clinker, II, 91, 172, 185.

171   TNA, RG 11/2239, 2242, 2358; *ibid.* MAF 68/486, 1626; SRO, A/BAZ 4/11; *Kelly's Dir. Som.* (1883); Mitchell, V. and Smith, K., *Taunton to Barnstaple* (Midhurst, 1995), unpag.

172   Wilts RO 2515/210, box 210/2, 10, 27-8; box 262/1; box 263/4-5; SRO, A/BAZ 4/11; Maggs, C., *The Taunton to Barnstaple Line*, 37-8; *Kelly's Dir. Som.* (1883, 1906); TNA, RG 12/1864, RG 13/2266.

173   *Exmoor Review*, 1996, 43-4.

174   Mitchell, V. and Smith, K., *Taunton to Barnstaple* (Midhurst, 1995), unpag.; Oakley, M., *Somerset Railway Stations* (2002), 52-3.

175   TNA, RG 13/2266; *Kelly's Dir. Som.*(1906).

CHAPTER 9 Exmoor in Living Memory, pp. 149-76

176   *Exmoor Review* (1970), 67-9.

177   TNA, MAF 68/2745, 2766, 3793, 3809; *Kelly's Dir. Devon* (1935); *Kelly's Dir. Som.* (1939).

178   SRO, D/P/dul 24/1/123; D/R/du 24/1/39, 59; DD/X/BRR 2; *Exmoor Review*, 1985, 23-4.

179   TNA, MAF 32/133/93; SRO, Exmoor Oral Archive; *ibid.* A/BAZ 2/9; Henriques, R., *Sir Robert Waley-Cohen, 1877-1952* (1966), 297-8, 377, 392, 402-5.

180   Farms were graded A, B or C according to how well managed they were. TNA, MAF 32/121/09; 32/131/91; 32/133/92-3; 32/164/99, 101; 32/667/323, 32/682/334; 32/700/342; 32/702/344.

181   TNA, MAF 32/667/323, 32/682/334; 32/700/342; 32/702/344; MAF 68/3793, 3809, 4161, 4177, 4547, 4974, 4997, 6002, 6024.

182   SRO, DD/KW 1947/8; DD/X/BID 11; D/P/dul 24/1/178; *ibid.* A/BAZ 2/6, 11-12; J.M.B. Mackie, 'Galloways on Exmoor', *Exmoor Review* (1960); H.R. Thomas, 'Hill farming on Exmoor', *Exmoor Review* (1982), 38-43.

183   Smith, M., *An Illustrated History of Exmoor's Railways*, 31-6.

184   SRO, DD/TBL 90/19; DD/OH 4/1; *ibid.* A/BAZ 2/16; A/CJN 1/3, 5; *ibid.* C/OP 9/8; TNA, MAF 68/4974, 4997, 6002, 6024; Som CC, HER.

185   SRO, DD/X/RID 10; *Exmoor Review*, 2002, 21; 2005, 34-5. The farmer at Broford refused to allow 920 cattle to be culled in 2001. www.guardian.co.uk/uk/2001/feb/28/footandmouth.foodanddrink (Accessed 21 Nov 08).

186   *Kelly's Dir. Som.* (1906, 1923, 1931, 1939); *Kelly's Dir. Devon* (1935); SRO, Exmoor Oral Archive.

187   SRO, D/R/du 3/1/6-7, 24/1/59, 121; *ibid.* A/BAZ 2/6, 11-12; *ibid.* Exmoor Oral Archive.

188   Som CC, HER; SRO, Exmoor Oral Archive; *Kelly's Dir. Som.* (1906, 1939).

189   Hawkins, M., *Somerset at War, 1939-1945* (Wimborne, 1988), 193, 195, 199; Som. CC, HER.

190   SRO, C/E 4/407/1; *ibid.* D/R/dul 3/1/2-3; DD/BS 8; *ibid.* Exmoor Oral Archives; Som. C.C., HER; Hawkins, M., *Somerset at War, 1939-1945* (Wimborne, 1988), 107, 118, 121, 193, 195, 199, 211-12.

191   SRO, DD/BS 13; Wilson, J., *The Somerset Home Guard* (Bath, 2004), 171-9.

192   SRO, Exmoor Oral Archive; *Kelly's Dir. Som.* (1906, 1939); SRO, D/R/dul 3/1/7-8; Exford school, log book 1923-79.

193   SRO, A/AGH 1/130, 151-2, 382, 386; *ibid.* D/R/dul 24/1/166-7, 171; *ibid.* Exmoor Oral Archive; *Exmoor Review*, 1963, 20-1.

194   Census.

195   Baron, R.S., *Westward Ho! From Cambria to Cornwall* (1934), 285.

196   *Exmoor Review* (1967).

197   MacEwen, M., *The Greening of a Red* (1991), 259-60.

198   Dower, J., *National Parks in England and Wales* (Ministry of Town and Country Planning (1945) (Cmd 6628); Hobhouse, A., *Report of the National Parks Committee (England and Wales)* (Ministry of Town and Country Planning (1947) (Cmd 7121); Hartley, D., *The Countryman's England* (1935); MacEwen, A. and MacEwen, M., *Greenprints for the Countryside: The Story of Britain's national parks* (1987).

199   DNB; Yeates, J., *An Endless View: the Artist and Exmoor* (Dulverton, 1995); SRO, Exmoor Oral Archive; Binding, H., Pearce, B., and Pugsley, S., *Exmoor Century* (Tiverton, 2001), *passim.*

200   Bonham-Carter, V., *Exmoor Writers and their Works* (Dulverton, 1987), passim.

201   *Kelly's Dir. Som.* (1923, 1939); SRO, Exmoor Oral archive.

PANELS

Panel 1

Riley, H. and Wilson-North, R., *The Field Archaeology of Exmoor* (English Heritage, 2001).

Panel 2

Donn's map of Devon 1765; Atkin, M.A., 'Places Named Anstey', *Journal of English Place Name Society* (30, 1997-8), 83, 89-90; Coates, R., Breeze, A. and Horovitz, D., *Celtic Voices, English Places: Studies of the Celtic Impact on Place Names in England* (Stamford, 2000), 294; Riley, H. and Wilson-North, R., *The Field Archaeology of Exmoor* (English Heritage, 2001), 80-1.

Panel 3

List descriptions of the churches can be found at www.imagesofengland.org.uk.

Panel 4

SRO, DD/AHT; DD/AH 11/9.

Panel 5

MacDermot, E.T., *A History of the Forest of Exmoor* (1973), 247-53, 293, 446-7, 450; SRO, DD/SF 1/2/24; D/P/wins 4/1/3; DD/S/HY 30; DD/DR 68; Winsford tithe award; Somerset CC, HER; TNA, C 1/765/34.

Panel 6

SRO DD/SP probate inventories.

Panel 7

SRO, A/CRZ 1/6; A/AKK 7; *ibid.* tithe awards Exford, Hawkridge, Winsford; Devon RO 1148M add 1/52; TNA, RG 10/2358A.

Panel 8

Unpublished Survey Report, 'Four Exmoor Farms', Keystone Historic Buidlings Consultants, report ref K727 (2007); notes to accompany reconstruction drawings, Allen Adams (2008); Barnwell, P.S. and Giles, C., *English Farmsteads, 1750-1914*, Swindon (1997), RCHME.

Panel 9

TNA ref RG 13/5060.

Panel 10

www.helm.org.uk/upload/pdf/Landscape-Legacy.pdf

Further Reading and Sources

Studying an area like Exmoor, which lies in two counties, means that resources need to be looked for in many different places.

Details of both printed and documentary sources, as well as additional information about the area can be found on the websites: www.victoriacountyhistory.ac.uk/Somerset and www.englandspastforeveryone.org.uk/Exmoor.

Original documents, maps and photographs are to be found at the Somerset, Devon or North Devon Record Offices in Taunton, Exeter and Barnstaple respectively. Secondary local sources are located at the West Country Studies Library in Exeter and the Somerset Studies Library in Taunton. There are further sources at the Exmoor National Park Authority and the Heritage Centre, both in Dulverton, Barnstaple Studies Library and North Devon Athenaeum, Barnstaple, and South Molton and District Archive. The National Archives at Kew and the British Library in London hold both national and local source material. English Heritage's National Monuments Record Centre in Swindon is particularly good for buildings research. Somerset's Historic Environment Record, giving details of archaeological sites from prehistory to the Cold War, and listed buildings, is also available on line.

Exmoor is rich in oral history archives, most of which are stored in the Somerset Record Office (SRO) in Taunton. Notes and transcripts can be found on the SRO website and a selection has been printed in Johnson, B. and Rattenbury, M.J., *Reflections: Life Portraits of Exmoor* (Dulverton, 2003).

There are many books on Exmoor for both background reading and detailed information on specific topics. The *Exmoor Review* contains articles of historical interest. Other important printed sources are the volumes of the Cornwall, Devon and Somerset Record Societies and the publications of local societies, such as the Somerset Archaeological and Natural History Society, many of which also have websites. Their publications will be found in most major local libraries. Books on Exmoor and historical sources in print can be found at the Somerset Studies Library in Taunton, the West Country Studies Library in Exeter, the Barnstaple Studies Library and North Devon Athenaeum, Barnstaple, and the Dulverton and South Molton libraries.

The Somerset Studies Library holds an important collection of printed sources for local history including printed Calendars

of Charter, Close, Fine and Patent Rolls, the Letters and Papers of
Henry VIII, the Acts of the Privy Council, State Papers, Inquisitions
Post Mortem, Book of Fees, Feudal Aids, Curia Regis Rolls, Ancient
Deeds, Committees for the Advance of Money and Compounding,
Papal Letters, and Treasury Books; the Taxation of Pope Nicholas,
and the *Valor Ecclesiasticus;* volumes of the Pipe Roll Society and
the Rolls Society notably the *Red Book of the Exchequer;* clergy lists
and diocesan directories, and biographies of university alumni and
Members of Parliament.

The Somerset Archaeological Society has an extensive collection
of books on national and local history, based in the Somerset
Studies Library in Taunton, including volumes of the Victoria
County History for several western counties; a substantial and up-
to-date collection of record society volumes and local periodicals
covering most of the country; printed surveys of agriculture;
18th- and 19th-century county histories; and a large collection
of topographical illustrations. In addition the Somerset Studies
Library and the West Country Studies Library hold directories,
maps, newspapers, books of old photographs, parish magazines
and other small printed items relating to local communities in
Somerset and Devon. Both county record offices also have small
libraries and collections of pamphlets, articles, and cuttings
relating to Exmoor.

The following is a list of useful books for a study of Exmoor
history, and others will be found in the notes to each chapter.

Bibliography

EARLY HISTORY

Darby, H.C., *The Domesday Geography of South-West England* (Cambridge, 1967)

Gover, J.E.B., Mawer, A. and Stenton, F.M. (eds.), *Place Names of Devon* (Cambridge, 1931-2)

Journals of English Place Name Society

Kain, R., *England's Landscape: The South West* (English Heritage, Swindon, 2006)

Riley H. and Wilson-North, R., *The Field Archaeology of Exmoor* (English Heritage, Swindon, 2001)

Smith, A.H., *English Place-Name Elements*, 2 vols. (Cambridge, 1956)

Thorn, C. and F., *Domesday Book: Devon* (Chichester, 1985)

Thorn, C. and F., *Domesday Book: Somerset* (Chichester, 1980)

Turner, S. (ed.), *Medieval Devon and Cornwall: Shaping an Ancient Countryside* (Macclesfield, 2006)

Turner, S., *Making a Christian Landscape* (Exeter, 2006)

EXMOOR FOREST

Chadwyck-Healey, C.E.H. (ed.), *Somersetshire Pleas c.1200-1256* (Somerset Record Society 11, Taunton, 1897)

MacDermot, E.T., *A History of the Forest of Exmoor* (1911; new edn, Newton Abbot, 1973)

Orwin, C.S. and Sellick, R.J., *The Reclamation of Exmoor Forest* (Newton Abbot, 1970)

Summerson, H. (ed.), *Crown Pleas of the Devon Eyre of 1238* (Devon and Cornwall Record Society, NS 28, Torquay, 1985)

MEDIEVAL AND EARLY MODERN EXMOOR

Chadwyck Healey, C.E.H. (ed.), *Bellum Civile: Hopton's Narrative of his Campaign in the West, 1642-4* (Somerset Record Society 18, Taunton, 1902)

Fenwick, C.C. (ed.), *The Poll Taxes of 1377, 1379, and 1381* (Oxford, 1998)

Howard, A.J. and Stoate, T.L. (ed.), *Somerset Protestation Returns* (Bristol, 1975)

Siraut, M. (ed.), *Somerset Wills* (Somerset Record Society 89, Taunton, 2003)

Stevens, D., *War and Peace in West Somerset 1620-1670* (Minehead, 1988)

Stoate, T.L. (ed.), *Devon Subsidy Rolls 1543-5* (Bristol, 1986)

Swete, J., *Travels in Georgian Devon*, T. Gray (ed.), III (Tiverton, 1999)

Underdown, D., *Revel, Riot, and Rebellion* (Oxford, 1987)

Weaver, F.W. (ed.), *Wells Wills* (1890)

Webb, A.J., *Two Tudor Subsidy Assessments* (Somerset Record Society 88, Taunton, 2002)

MODERN EXMOOR

Acland, T.D. and Sturge, W., *The Farming of Somersetshire* (1851)

Billingsley, J., *General View of Agriculture of Somerset* (Bath, 1798)

Binding, H. and Bonham-Carter, V., *Old Dulverton and around* (Dulverton, 1986)

Bonham-Carter, V., *Exmoor Writers and their Works* (Dulverton, 1987)

Burt, R., Waite, P. and Burnley R., *Devon and Somerset Mines* (Exeter, 1984)

First Report on Agricultural Depression: Report by Assistant Commissioner on North Devon (C-7728) HC (1894)

Harley, J.B. and Dunning, R.W. (ed.), *Somerset Maps* (Somerset Record Society 76, Taunton, 1981)

Hawkins, M., *Somerset at War, 1939-1945* (Wimborne, 1988)

Mitchell, V. and Smith, K., *Taunton to Barnstaple* (Midhurst, 1995)

Report of the Royal Commission on Children, Young Persons, and Women in Agriculture (Parliamentary Papers, 1868-9 (4202))

Symons, W., *Early Methodism in West Somerset and the Lorna Doone Country* (1895)

Vancouver, C., *General View of the agriculture of the County of Devon with observations on the means of its improvement* (1808)

Yeates, J., *An Endless View: the Artist and Exmoor* (Dulverton, 1995)

Index

Picture Credits

The authors and publishers wish to thank the following for permission to reproduce their material. Any infringement of copyright is entirely accidental: every care has been taken to contact or trace all copyright owners. We would be pleased to correct in future editions any errors or omissions brought to our attention. References are to page numbers except where stated.

Bayeux Museum, France, 37, 43

Bridgeman Art Library, 170 (Fig. 110)

Bristol News & Media, 6, 121, 148

British Museum (The Trustees of), 25

Christie's Images Ltd, 126

English Heritage: (© Crown Copyright, NMR), 145, 159 (Fig. 104), (Allan T. Adams), 130, 131, 132, 133, (Images of England), 66

Exmoor National Park Authority, 5, 16, 17, 31, 40 (Fig. B), 42, 51, 72, 74, 89 (Fig. 53), 92, 97 (Fig. 58), 102, 111, 113, 114, 122, 124, 143, 161, 165, 168, 169

Getty Images (John Turlton/Hulton Archive) 9, (Fox Photos/ Hulton Archive), 151, 153, (Popperfoto), 158

Hampton and Teddington Post, 172 (Fig. 113)

Andrew Jones, Vicar of Bishops Nympton and Molland, 144

Anne Leaver, 10, 14, 18, 20, 27

Dr Gareth Morgan, 171

Munning Trustees, Dedham, Essex, 170 (Fig. 111)

Royal Albert Memorial Museum and Art Gallery, Exeter, 22

Somerset Archaeological and Natural History Society, 40 (Fig. A), 62, 63, 99 (Fig. 62), 103, 128, 172 (Fig. 114), 173

Somerset County Council (Historic Environment Record), 61, 110, 126

Somerset County Museum, 32, 44, 93

Somerset Record Office, 38, 55, 56, 70, 80, 85, 89 (Fig. 52), 93 (Fig. C), 104, 106, 109, 115, 138, 139, 140, 146, 150, 152, 155, 156, 159 (Fig. 103), 160, (John Lyddon Pring), 56 (Fig. 32), 75, 135, (With thanks to the depositors), 68, 86, 96 (Fig. 57), 118

The National Archives, 90, 97 (Fig. 59), 136

University of London, xii, 2, 5, 7, 12, 28, 35, 48, 57, 59, 65, 73, 79, 81, 82, 83, 96 (Fig. 56), 98, 99 (Fig. 61), 101, 112, 116, 119, 127, 137, 141, 142, 162, 175

The following maps were drawn by Cath D'Alton © University of London, (Figs 2, 4, 11, 51, Panel 2: Fig. A, 23, 27, 29, 108).